AMERICAN RACISM

AND WHAT YOU CAN DO ABOUT IT

The Hard Truth About America and Americans

DONALD L. SCOTT

STRATTON
—PRESS—

Publishing Life

American Racism and What You Can Do About It
Copyright © 2020 **Donald L. Scott**

Stratton Press Publishing
831 N Tatnall Street Suite M #188,
Wilmington, DE 19801
www.stratton-press.com
1-888-323-7009

ISBN (Paperback): 978-1-64895-074-2
ISBN (Hardback): 978-1-64895-076-6
ISBN (Ebook): 978-1-64895-075-9

Printed in the United States of America

To Betty J. Scott,
1938–2019,
the wind beneath my wings for fifty-seven years.

PREFACE

THIS BOOK TELLS THE HARD truths of America's Founding Documents, written in 1776 and 1787 for white Americans and their future generations. Hard truths bring pain but are necessary for people to take the proper actions to correct the correctable and live with the uncorrectable. The God of the universe and of mankind is included in my assessment of hard truths Americans must confront to end institutional racism.

Most white Americans don't like to talk about white supremacy or racism. Most African Americans seethe with anger over having been enslaved and excluded from the protections of the founding documents. Native Americans have never forgotten the seizure of their lands and broken promises of treaties and confiscation of mineral rights. Other minorities are not as vocal about their exclusion and protections of the documents, but the sting of discrimination remains in their collective memory. Thankfully, a few white Americans inserted their belief that all men were created equal in the Declaration of Independence that allowed white Americans of character, over time, to amend the Constitution (the governing document) and include people of color. Fortunately, most white Americans are not racists. I think most are apathetic to the issues that affect minorities. Inspired by protests led by racial minority, a few elected white leaders rise above institutional racism that favors their race to dismantle the most egregious laws that denied equal opportunities to people of color.

The sensitivity of racial issues with all Americans require an approach toward discussion without malice toward the founders but with profound gratitude for the adjustments made since 1865 to dismantle some of the most restrictive laws negatively impacting nonwhite Americans. I believe my credibility to speak about racism is acceptable to most Americans. And I boldly share my views about the evolution of *American racism and what we can do about it.*

My experience with American racism spans over eighty years and prepared me to share insights and observations of the white majority's rule in America. I have been among the African American recipients of the 1954 Supreme Court decision era to integrate white organizations, schools, and neighborhoods and among the first eighty-five African Americans promoted to general officer rank in the US Army. I entered the army as a second lieutenant in 1960 and retired as a brigadier general in 1991. After the end of the Vietnam War, the army successfully reviewed policies and programs to remove institutional racism from assignment and promotion criteria, mandated race relation classes for all career military and civilian personnel, and included diversity training for sergeant and officer development courses. Insights and observations from that experience proved valuable in my postmilitary career. After retirement from the army, I was appointed by Maynard Jackson, mayor of Atlanta, and confirmed by the Atlanta City Council as chief of staff and later as the chief operating officer of the city. As the mayor's chief of staff, I coordinated his direct reports in all areas of community outreach and political concerns with county, state, and federal officials. And as chief operating officer, I managed the daily operations of the city's delivery of services to include oversight of Atlanta's International Airport. Mayor Jackson's unique cooperation between Atlanta's corporate leaders and the black and white community leaders produced prosperity, tranquility, and goodwill. My Atlanta experience helped me win senior executive appointments in both the executive and legislative branches of the federal government. As the founding director of AmeriCorps National Civilian Community Corps, a residential

National Service program, I designed the program, hired and trained staff, and recruited eighteen- to twenty-four-year-old racially and gender diverse youths to respond to disaster relief and other unmet needs in American communities—the program is in its twenty-fifth year of operation. I was appointed Deputy Librarian of Congress by the Librarian of Congress and confirmed by the US Senate to manage the daily operations and resolve decades old racial discrimination law suits against the institution. My ten-year interface with congressional oversight committees provided opportunities to evaluate congressional response to issues of race based upon the diversity of the district they represent.

I share my credentials not to boast or impress but to emphasize that my opportunities were made possible by white American's who dismantled or passed laws providing African Americans the opportunities afforded all Americans. From these experiences came observations, insights, and recommendations to minimize race and promote the equality of the Declaration of Independence and rights under the US Constitution. The Declaration of Independence is America's antidote against the negative effects of white supremacy.

I'll discuss the political, educational, religious, and business systems were purposely designed to favor the white Americans. The self-evident truths about all men being created equal recorded in the Declaration of Independence by the founding fathers of America are not evident to most Americans. Thomas Jefferson, the author of the document and third president of America, was known to believe that African slaves were intellectually inferior to whites but entered the phrase without qualification to race or gender.

Abraham Lincoln and the rebirth of freedom following the Civil War marks the beginning of a series of hard truths that begun corrections to include African Americans under the protection of the US Constitution. And like most good deeds, opportunities gained by blacks under the Constitution were fiercely attacked by advocates of white supremacy. Harry Truman and Thurgood Marshall, Earl Warren and Dwight Eisenhower, and John Kennedy and Lyndon Johnson delivered hard truths that further amended the

Constitution to reflect the nation's promise stated in the Declaration of Independence.

America is a very young country, and each new generation must continue to keep racism or any other factionalism from making laws that nullify the meaning and purpose of the Declaration of Independence. Among my suggestions in *What You Can Do about It* (keeping America true to the Declaration of Independence) is the story of how the United Army and other uniformed services became America's most respected organization for honesty, opportunity, and efficiency. You'll find useful tips to guide you, your family, and friends in ways to keep America strong on your watch. I hope you enjoy as much as I do being a citizen of the most respected and unique country on planet earth. My status as an American of African descent make me proud of all Americans who rose above local prejudice to honor our commitment to equality for all under the one and only Declaration of Independence on planet earth. Good luck, God bless in keeping America true to her DNA—the Declaration of Independence.

INTRODUCTION

AMERICAN RACISM IS GRANDIOSE, COMPLEX, and unique because the founding of the country was all of that and more. The founding documents, the DNA of the country, presents a statement about America's belief that all people are created equal, but the seeds of white supremacy built a Constitution/government of the people that did not enfranchise racial minorities and women. Not a good start. For centuries, the Declaration of Independence has been the source of power to dismantle the laws that discriminate on the basis of race, gender, or national origin to align the nations governing documents with the American purpose. This tug of war between the two documents produces sentiments of white supremacy in every generation of Americans that require the better angels to educate and eradicate its influence on the equality of governance and opportunity for all. I have been fortunate enough to live through the dismantling of racial segregation laws that were replaced by integration of public schools, civil and voting rights, and equal employment opportunities. My insight and observation of the white majority during this period shaped my understanding of why Americans are continually dealing with institutional racism and what each American can do to eradicate it from our governance and national psyche. Acknowledging the hard truths of racism is the first step toward eradication.

July 4, 2019, marked the 243rd anniversary of America, and American racism still dominates our national headlines. Americans are still complaining, denying, and ignoring that our beloved country is racist. The loudest voices come from the three racial groups that have been together since before America severed all ties as a British colony and declared its independence. White Americans are uncomfortable talking about the subject, black Americans are the most vocal about the subject, Native Americans continually challenge the US government over their sovereignty. Hispanics are the latest focus of immigration on our southern border, and claims of racism dominate the issue. These flash points all have their roots in the persistent efforts of some white politicians who fan the emotions of their racial group to use the laws to restrict racial minorities' voting rights in the country. To the credit of the white majority most appeals for white supremacy have failed. Yet they never give up. As the demographic shifts in America and whites become the minority racial group, a greater understanding of the importance of preserving the rule of law needs to happen. And I think my insight and experience as an American of African descent can help educate and prepare all Americans to remain true to the intent and purpose of the Declaration and the US Constitution regardless of the racial demographics.

I have been blessed to experience, prosper, and learn from those who dismantled laws and/or made amendments to the Constitution that benefited all citizens. By any measure of success, I have had a remarkable career (brigadier general, United States Army; chief operating officer, City of Atlanta, Georgia; founding director, AmeriCorps National Civilian Community Corps [NCCC]; and Deputy Librarian of the Library of Congress). My journey, like America's, had beautiful peaks and dangerous swamps but was always guided by the north star of the Declaration, the amended US Constitution, and the rule of law.

My observations and insights gained from my career were learned from a racially diverse group of Americans, where whites were in the majority and all were dedicated to mission accomplishment while upholding the highest ideals of the American brand: the Declaration and the US Constitution. I have met a few white supremacists held in check by the laws and public opinion. Unfortunately, I have met many Americans of all racial groups apathetic to the toxic effects of American racism that continue to deny a racial group benefits and opportunities available to every other American. Apathy favors the loudest voices for denying rights to minorities of gender, sex, or race.

My use of the term *white supremacy* refers to those who supported discriminatory laws in the past and who continue to support them in the present. Regrettably, some white Americans will find my use of the term misplaced, and most Americans will not agree with my characterization of apathy among their numbers. My purpose is to inspire and not offend because like-minded Americans from each racial group are the key to dismantling institutional racism and protecting the rule of law. This action is urgent and necessary regardless of the race or ethnicity of the incumbent president.

This book will provide you a clear understanding of the tensions and purpose between the Declaration of Independence and the Constitution of the United States. You will see that both the Declaration and Constitution must be kept in harmony to protect America's unique brand of a nation of excellence for all of its citizens. You will also learn the language to talk about race and civility to work for the common good of "We the People." And best of all, you will learn how to stop institutional racism by consciously identifying your allegiance to America over your identity with your racial group.

Preparing for and writing this book has helped me to better understand the country of my birth. Accepting the unflattering truth of my ancestor's bondage and exclusion from "We the People" in the Declaration of Independence is a truth toward belonging, inclusion, forgiving, and loving. I hope all Americans accept the truth of our exclusion at the founding and work together to make the two documents the glue to bind all Americans together and, more importantly, work together to preserve our unique American brand. You may surprise yourself as I did. I have come to admire and respect George Washington, our first president, slave owner and supporter of white supremacy. He made amends for his inhumanity by freeing his slaves upon his death. Washington's farewell address embodies the high principles of humanity, and his sage advice on preserving the fledgling democracy was as appropriate now as it was in 1789. I think you, too, will agree that the measure of a person is where they stand in controversy in the midst of peers who disagree with their action on matters of critical importance. Abraham Lincoln, Harry Truman, Dwight Eisenhower, John Kennedy, and Lyndon Johnson, along with Supreme Court Chief Justice Earl Warren and Associate Justice Thurgood Marshall (earned distinction as legal strategist for the NAACP)—all had the courage to blend the Declaration with the Constitution.

PART 1

America's DNA: Born in Crisis, Established in Controversy, Blemished by Slavery

THINK ON THIS FOR THE remainder of your life. America was born in crisis, and the founding fathers declared independence from Great Britain in 1776 with the noble announcement of forming a new nation that believed that all men were created equal and endowed by their creator with certain inalienable rights. The Declaration of Independence starts with these lofty words that became the DNA of American identity. These same farsighted founders crafted the US Constitution to develop a government of the people, by the people, and for the people that protected the interests of slave owners at the expense of the Declaration of Independence. African slaves and Native Americans were not in the portrait of "We the People." The seeds of white supremacy in the drafting of the Constitution protecting slavery influenced the admission of every state that joined the Union and American territories. Worst, the laws passed to protect slavery eroded the assertion that all men were created equal in the new government of the United States. Despite the flaws, America became and is the only planet on earth to stipulate a belief in God and nature's God that all men are created equal. This belief has made America the most favored destination for people facing persecution or wanting the freedoms offered by the American

Constitution. Americans in the twenty-first century must take note and eliminate institutional racism to protect our unique nation.

The Civil War, Reconstruction, and Civil Rights eras have not erased it from America. Ask yourself the question: what can I do to eradicate it?

This is a hard truth and critical question that must be embraced and answered without malice for the sins and injustices of/to our ancestors and damage to the Declaration of Independence. We now know that each generation of Americans must embrace the past, answer the question, and act to protect our American DNA, the Declaration of Independence.

CHAPTER ONE

The Declaration of Independence: America's Remarkable and Unique DNA

I N THE SWELTERING SUMMER AT Philadelphia in 1776, America's DNA as a new nation was being formed. Thomas Jefferson, the principal author of the Declaration of Independence,[1] prominent slave owner, brilliant man of letters, an advocate of white superiority, boldly stated the proposition that all men were created equal without equivocation or qualification. He knew African slaves were human because he fathered children by a multiracial slave and half-sister of his wife. Nevertheless, Jefferson was known for his belief that African slaves were inferior to the white race but refrained or was restrained from limiting God's creation to only the white race in the most cherished document of America, the Declaration of Independence. Perhaps the numerous revisions and edits by the drafting committee and the full committee wanted to use language that was compatible with the Bible and their belief that God was on their side.[2] I'll grant the good Lord's intersession in their purpose for the sake of posterity. The remarkable fact remains that the original document pub-

---

[1] "Declaration of Independence," Wikipedia, last modified September 28, 2019, https://en.wikipedia.org/wiki/United_States_Declaration_of_Independence.

[2] James A. Hutson, "Religion and the Founding of the American Republic," (Washington, DC: Library of Congress, 1998), https://lccn.loc.gov/2003557109.

lished on the morning of July 4, 1776, survives unchanged unto this moment. The sentiment expressed in the opening paragraphs of the document places the Declaration in the sacred category as the Bible.

Not all who profess to be Christians practice the beliefs demanded by Jesus Christ. Not all Americans know that America was founded on the proposition "that all men are created equal, that they are endowed by their Creator with certain unalienable Rights, that among these are Life, Liberty and the pursuit of Happiness." Many who know don't practice it. Both sacred documents require faith, commitment, and resolution to make sure the deeds of individuals reflect the organizations they represent: the church and the United States of America respectively. Both the church and the Constitution[3] have been used to justify violations of human rights by unjust men. Jefferson and the founders of the Declaration announced to the world the unjust treatment by Britain that inspired them to establish America and their bold experiment with democracy.

Their noble document ushered in the drafting of the United States Constitution with its "we the people" preamble and seeds of white supremacy that damaged the credibility of the Declaration of Independence for over a hundred years.

---

[3]   "The United States Constitution," US Constitution (website), last modified March 6, 2011, https://usconstitution.net/const.html.

CHAPTER TWO

Out of Philadelphia: The Constitution and Seeds of White Supremacy

OST AMERICANS KNOW THAT GEORGE Washington, John Adams, Thomas Jefferson, James Madison, Alexander Hamilton, and Ben Franklin played important roles in the founding of America. The name and deeds of Gouverneur Morris,[4] delegate from Pennsylvania by way of New York, is little known. He was not on center stage during the constitutional convention but played a significant role at the end of a fractious debate between delegates that crafted a remarkable new government embedded with the seeds of white supremacy. Gouverneur Morris and the more widely known Alexander Hamilton are representative of the small number of abolitionists who lost the effort to abolish slavery but managed to insert language that could include the slave at some future time in America's future. It is also helpful to understand that white men in the eighteenth century believed themselves superior to other races in the world. For that reason, creating a government with a belief that all are created equal set expectations among some delegates that a new governing document would support that lofty belief. The delib-

---

4   "Gouverneur Morris," Wikipedia, last modified February 1, 2001, https:// en.wikipedia.org/wiki/Gouverneur_Morris

erations would record that delegates were tied to traditions, fortunes, and cultural realities more than humanitarian, or moral, issues.

Fifty-five delegates representing all the states except Rhode Island met from May to September 1778 to write a workable Constitution. Many thought it was an improbable task as the state politicians did not want to give up their political power and state sovereignty to a more powerful central government. Most of the movers and shakers were present; Washington was unanimously elected president of the second Continental Congress, Madison of Virginia was a principal advocate for a strong central government, and Franklin, the peace broker, during heated debates was a busy man. Jefferson and Adams were out of the country but aware of the high stakes and importance to the survival of the fledging country and future of the United States.

Visions of Governance

The delegates from Virginia, New Jersey, and Hamilton of New York had a plan and vision of how the central government should be organized and exercise its power. Virginia seized the opportunity and made the opening presentation that stoked the worst fears of the smaller states. Virginia's vision was a government with three branches—legislative, executive, and judicial—with each branch independent and checking on each other. The states would give up their sovereignty to the central government. The delegates from the smaller states were so riled, they spent ten days debating the plan. New Jersey sharing the fears and concerns of the small states called only for a revision of the Articles of Confederation to enable the Congress more easily to raise revenues and regulate commerce. It also provided for acts of Congress and ratified treaties be "the supreme law of the States." The smaller states rallied around this plan, but the plan was defeated by a majority vote. Madison of Virginia understood the opposition to a powerful centralized government and persuaded the delegates to agree that any new constitution should be ratified through conventions of the people and not by the Congress and the state legislatures. He had done his homework and knew that the legislatures would likely deny the centralized power of a federal government to protect their political power within the state and federal system of government.

With Virginia's plan still on the table, Hamilton presented his vision of a strong federal government in detailing how it would exercise power-conjured fears of the return of a British monarchy. The delegates, weary of the debates of a weak or strong central government, began to explore the issues of concern to their states.

Clash of Interests

Commerce and taxation dominated the interests of the delegates. Both the northern and southern states had delegates from small states and large states that could turn a phrase and protect their state's interest. Yet compromise was the pathway to progress. The small states lost the first battle when the convention approved a resolution that established population as the basis of representation in the House of Representatives. The small states tried to get equal representation in the Senate, but a tie vote spoiled their effort and the large-state delegates refused to compromise. This nearly ended the convention, but the trade-offs continued with the southern states securing their interests in the method used to count slaves for purposes of taxation and representation. The delegates agreed that the representation and taxation in the house would be the number of white inhabitants and three-fifths of the "other people"—a euphemism for slaves. Gouverneur Morris strongly opposed slavery and any euphemism used to assist its existence. The delegates rolled on.

With goodwill prevalent, a Committee of Detail drew up the draft Constitution. The delegates poured over the contents, and when delegates got to the section on commerce, emotions erupted among the north and south members again. The southern states exported a lot of raw materials, rice, indigo, and tobacco and feared that a New England–dominated Congress might impose export taxes that would severely damage the South's economic life. The issue became linked with slavery again. Martin of Maryland proposed a tax on slave importation, and the issue accelerated into a discussion on the institution of slavery and it's moral and economic relationship to the new government.

The southern delegates defended slavery as a business interest, and the northern delegates sought to dismantle slavery as a moral issue. Rutledge of South Carolina, in response to the negative impact as a moral issue on the Constitution and the new government, asserted that slavery had nothing at all to do with morality and declared, "Interest alone is the governing principle with nations." Congregationalist minister and abolitionist Samuel Hopkins of Connecticut berated the convention for supporting slavery. He asked, "How does it appear…that States, who have been fighting for liberty and consider themselves as the highest and most noble example of zeal for it, cannot agree in any political Constitution unless it indulge and authorize them to enslave their fellow men…" Any hope for killing the institution of slavery was lost. Slavery as an interest would rule the argument over slavery as a moral issue for eighty years.

Political compromise was reached on commerce issues, including slavery, when the delegates from South Carolina and Georgia reached agreement with the delegates from the New England States to extend slave importation for twenty years. The southerner's accepted a clause in exchange that required only a simple majority vote on navigation laws, which meant a crippling blow to southern economic interests. The only remaining issue was the method of electing the president.

Significant Changes

Four months of defending and promoting their states in the creation of a new Constitution to represent their states best interest left the delegates weary. Nevertheless, proposals for electing the executive included direct election by the people, by state legislatures, by state governors, and by the new government. The solution included all the players. The Electoral College was thought up as a way to distribute the decision-making process while ensuring the new government had final choice over the selection of the president. The large states got proportional strength in the number of delegates, the state legislatures got the right to select the delegates, and the house the right to choose the president in the event that no candidate received a majority of the electoral votes. How the delegates came up with this expedient solution can only be attributed to their collective belief that politicians are smarter than the people they represent. The delegates were anxious to go home and selected a Committee of Style and Arrangement. Gouverneur Morris, highly regarded for his keen intellect, respected by George Washington, originally from New York and delegate from Pennsylvania, was selected to finalize the document.

The Expansion of America's Mission and Purpose

The opening preamble on the draft given to Morris by the Committee simply stated that we the people of the states of (the thirteen states) do ordain, declare, and establish the following constitution for the government of ourselves and our posterity. In just three days, Morris reframed the document from establishing a confederation of states without overarching purpose, to a document creating a nation with powerful goals. Morris reframed it to read "We, the People of the United States, in order to form a more perfect union, to establish justice, insure domestic tranquility, provide for the common defense, promote the general welfare, and secure the blessings of liberty to ourselves and our posterity, do ordain and establish the Constitution for the United States of America." The delegates raised no objections to the change and gladly approved the documents. The document was printed on September 17, 1787, and set in motion a larger debate and ratification by the states. Although Morris was unsuccessful keeping the euphemisms that supported slavery out of the Constitution, he made it harder for the supporters of slavery to deny that African slaves were under the sovereignty of the new Constitution of the United States. The language also envisioned adding more states and including a diverse citizenry of men and women created equally by their Creator. Gouverneur Morris was a visionary.

The Completed Constitution: Flawed by Slavery

The creation of the Constitution with the sanction of the majority of the most respected white men in business, politics, and religion refusing to acknowledge African slaves as part of "We the People" can only be explained by their embrace of white supremacy. Fortunately, there were respected white men in the above group who wanted to end slavery on moral grounds. However, there is no evidence that the abolitionist would have made the male slave an equal to the white male and a part of "We the People" in the Constitution. George Washington, the respected general, president, and statesman, and a slave owner, also left a legacy that can be interpreted that he was a man of conscience about the issue of slavery. He freed the slaves he owned upon his death with a stipulation of enactment. They couldn't exercise their freedom until his wife, Martha Washington, died. So many unexplained incidents happened at Mount Vernon after George died (buildings mysteriously catching fire, etc.) that Martha feared George's slaves were trying to kill her so they could be free. She set them free so she could be free of the anxiety. The Washington's complex relationship with American slavery would be experienced by a generation of slave holders. And George Washington as the father of America published his farewell suggestions to Americans on topics of concern for the future of the country. Slavery was not mentioned in the letter nor addressed by him in any public statements. His last will and testament provide the best insight on what he thought about his slaves in particular.

CHAPTER THREE

George Washington Set the Standard for
Accepting the Institution of Slavery

B OLD ADVENTURES AND BIG IDEAS need a hero with a résumé
larger than life, unquestioned by those he leads. George
Washington was the ideal person to serve as the country's first
president. In his time, George Washington was the go-to guy of his
era. Tall and erect, standing over seventy-six inches tall, immacu-
lately attired in military uniform, solid reputation for character and
integrity, as well as a devout believer in prayer and providence, he
was the full package. He was the unanimous choice for every critical
leadership role in the brash, upstart colonies of America who had
the gall to drop the word *colony* from their identity and just become
America. By all accounts, George Washington delivered in every post
to which he was appointed or elected. Successful and victorious general of the Continental Army over the British Army and Navy, unanimous choice for the presidency of America, and served two terms as
president. He was begged to serve a third term but declined. He was
humble to a fault and always downplayed his qualification to hold
the high offices his peers unanimously elected him for.

Washington was popular for his sound judgement, dependabil-
ity, and courage. Men of keen intellect was attracted to him probably because he valued knowledge that he did not possess. Alexander

Hamilton and James Madison shared his preference for a strong federal government and helped him write his farewell address[5] at the end of his presidency. Thomas Jefferson, secretary of state and the founder of the Democratic-Republican Party, was a fierce opponent of Alexander Hamilton, secretary of treasury and founder of the Federalist Party. Washington accepted a second term to keep the feud between Jefferson and Hamilton from tearing the new country apart. The feud and fragility of the federal government compelled Washington to caution the citizens about the dangers to the American government guided by its new Constitution. Some of his suggestions and cautions to the Americans of 1797 are relevant to Americans of 2020.

He urged Americans to place their identity as Americans above their identities as members of a state, city, or region and to focus their efforts and affection on the country above all interests. And regarding foreign influence, Washington argues that political parties must be restrained in a popularly elected government because of their tendency to distract the people from their own best interests, promote jealously among groups, and provide foreign nations and interests access to the government where they can impose their will upon the country. The Russian meddling in the American presidential election of 2016 makes George Washington a prophet. Yet Washington never publicly mentioned or wrote one word about the one topic that would plague America's domestic tranquility for 243 years: American racism. Why would a devout man of religion, supporter of the belief that all men were created equal, and the leader of America not comment on the divisive issue of slavery in his farewell address?

To comment on things you are unwilling to change because of their importance to your lively hood is to risk personal ruin. Perhaps Washington's reason for not making any public or written comments about slavery's threat to the domestic tranquility of America and its future will never be known. Speculation about his silence on the issue does not alter the inhuman treatment of enslaved Africans and the turbulent years of enforcing harsh laws to keep slaves under con-

---

5   "George Washington's Farewell Address," Wikipedia, last modified, January 8, 2011, https://en.wikipedia.org/wiki/George_Washington%27s_Farewell_Address.

trol. Washington's approval of the provisions to legalize slavery in the Constitution clearly signaled his support of the institution and its importance to America's future. Amazingly he distinguished himself from other white supremacists of his era by freeing his slaves in his last will and testament. His stipulation and timing of their freedom highlighted the dilemma between using slaves as a *species of property*, a term used by Washington for the wealth they represented over treating them as individuals with inalienable rights of freedom, liberty, and the pursuit of happiness. His 123 slaves were to be given their freedom upon the death of his wife, Martha Washington. His gesture created other problems for Martha but showed his good intention to correct his injustice to humanity through his enslavement of Africans.

Washington's ownership of slaves and releasing them from enslavement at his death were rarely mentioned in the storied celebration of his life that dominated American politics until the US Civil War. Ironically the interests of slave owners to carry their species of property to new states and territories was the dominant issue that lead to the Civil War. The white supremacy flaw in the Constitution that legalized slavery would grow and poison the very goals it was established to perform. By the time Abraham Lincoln would assume the presidency of "We the White People" in 1860, the American government under the Constitution had failed to form a more perfect union, establish justice, insure domestic tranquility, provide for the common defense, promote the general welfare, and secure the blessings of liberty for themselves and their posterity.

PART II

Cracks in the Union and Abe Lincoln's
New Birth of Freedom

HARD TRUTH NUMBER 2: THE institution of slavery was a well-thought-out, profit-driven system. It embedded the practice of white supremacy in the treatment of enslaved Africans and marginalized their humanity. Slave owners, banks, insurance companies, universities, and corporations were heavily invested in the system. White European and American investors selected the Africans to be enslaved for the hard labor in hot climates for two primary reasons: Africans were acclimated to working and living in hot weather, and the vast seas made it impossible for their escape and return to Africa. Their black skin color was an added bonus that made it difficult for them to blend in with the white population. They were counted as three-fifth of a person in the congressional district of their enslavement to advantage the southern vote in congress. The sinister assignment of dollar amounts by age, size, and sex reduced the slave to chattel property to be brought, worked, and sold for the profit of the owner. All children and family members were employed or sold in the manner most profitable to the owner. The profit motive demanded low overhead; clothing, housing, and food were rarely above subsistence levels. Education was forbidden, and health care was the responsibility of the slave community. The slave owner was the sole judge, jury, and executor over the lives of his property. White supremacists designed and enforced the all-out attack against the personhood of the enslaved African during slavery. The stain of racial discrimination is embedded in American culture.

American public attitudes and policy continue to be influenced by the history of slavery. Every time you hear a racist slur or see a concentration of poor blacks or poor whites in a geographical area, the residue of slavery is probably a contributing factor.

CHAPTER FOUR

Slavery and the Cracks in the Union

T HE INSTITUTION OF SLAVERY WENT through a crescendo of events before erupting into all-out Civil War between the states. Remember, the compromise between the southern and northern states over the issue of slavery allowed the states to be bound together as one nation under the new US Constitution. Between the time Washington ended his presidency and Lincoln[6] started his presidency, the issue of slavery, like a ball of yarn, unraveled the fragile cohesion between the northern and southern states in the union. The Southern Supporters of Slavery (SSS) favored states' rights and used every opportunity to make every territory desiring to join the union a slave state. The SSS blatantly enforced practices of white supremacy in the slave states to keep the enslaved Africans intimidated and under control. The abolitionist used every moral argument to oppose the expansion of slavery while attempting to abolish it from the US Constitution and America. What follows is a primer on the significant events that split the union, severely crippled the institution of slavery, and challenged President Lincoln to deal with the confederates, the enslaved, and the concept of America that strayed from the Declaration of Independence.

---

6   Carl Sandburg, Abraham Lincoln: The Prairie Years and the War Years (San Diego, CA: Harcourt, Brace, and World, 1939).

Missouri Compromise of 1821[7]

When Missouri petitioned to join the union as a slave state in 1821, United States senators from the north blocked their admission because power would shift to the southern states in the US Senate. To maintain parity in the senate, Maine was admitted as a free state and Missouri as a slave state. The US Congress also agreed to limit the spread of slavery north of latitude 36°30', excluding Missouri and the territory of Arkansas. The Missouri Compromise was thought by abolitionist in the US Congress to stop the expansion of slavery westward and usher in the death of slavery in the US. To the southern slave supporters (SSS), the compromise was just a temporary setback; their worst fears were realized when a slave rebellion broke out in Southern Virginia in 1831.

Nat Turner's Rebellion, August 1831[8]

Like a shock wave that spread through the slave-holding south, Nat Turner, a slave in Southern Virginia, organized a slave revolt and killed around sixty white people in two days of terror. The deployment of militia infantry and artillery aided in capturing Turner and fifty-five slaves. They were tried and executed for their role in the insurrection. Nearly two hundred more slaves in Virginia were lynched by crazed mobs in retaliation for Turner's revolt. Rigid laws were enforced throughout the slave-holding states curtailing the few freedoms free blacks and enslaved Africans enjoyed.

---

[7] "Missouri Compromise," Wikipedia, last modified January 9, 2013, https://en.wikipedia.org/wiki/Missouri_Compromise.

[8] "Nat Turner's slave rebellion," Wikipedia, last modified May 4, 2014, https://en.wikipedia.org/wiki/Nat_Turner%27s_slave_rebellion.

The War with Mexico and Wilmot Proviso, 1846–1850[9]

The SSS (Southern Supporters of Slavery) welcomed Texas as a slave state in 1845, and President Polk successfully urged the US Congress to authorize use of military force to punish Mexico as an excuse to seize New Mexico and California as American territories. President Polk achieved his goals of adding New Mexico and California as American territories, and the SSS sought to add them as slave states. Their efforts were blocked by David Wilmot, Republican, Pennsylvania, who introduced legislation at the close of the Mexican-American War to outlaw slavery in territory acquired by Texas, New Mexico, and California. The SSS and Democrats in Congress outmaneuvered the Republicans and introduced the concept of popular sovereignty that allowed the people in the territory to decide whether the state would become a slave or free state. The issue became so contested that the SSS in Congress began to talk about seceding from the union.

Fugitive Slave Compromise of 1850[10]

The compromise of 1850 attempted to reconcile SSS interests with northern abolitionists' efforts to abolish slavery. The major bills passed by the Thirty-First US Congress was to admit California as a free state while the remaining portions of the Mexican Cession were organized into New Mexico Territory and Utah Territory. Under the concept of popular sovereignty, the people of each territory would decide whether or not slavery would be permitted in those territories. The 1850 Fugitive Law amended the Fugitive Slave Law of 1793 by mandating under the penalty of law that individuals in free states return fugitive slaves to their owners. The original law enforced Article 4, Section 2, Clause 3 of the United States Constitution and directed the authorities in free states to return fugitive slaves to their

---

[9]   "Wilmot Proviso," Wikipedia, last modified March 14, 2019, https://en.wikipedia.org/wiki/Wilmot_Proviso.

[10] "Fugitive Slave Act of 1793," Wikipedia, last modified February 1, 2001, https://en.wikipedia.org/wiki/Fugitive_Slave_Act_of_1850.

masters. That law was not effective. Many of the authorities in border and free states passed "personal liberty laws" mandating a jury trial before alleged fugitive slaves could be moved; others forbade the use of local jails or the assistance of state officials in the arrest or return of alleged fugitive slaves. The 1850 amendment outraged northern citizens and influenced the expansion of the Underground Railroad—the network of white antislavery citizens providing hiding places for escaped slaves, making their way from slave states to free states. Approximately two hundred slaves were escaping at the time the law was passed, and the number increased significantly in the years following its passage. Slave owners hired slave catchers to go to popular destinations for escaped slaves in free states to return them back to captivity. Ohio and Michigan were popular destinations, and many escaped slaves continued on to Canada, out of reach of the slave catchers. The 1850 Fugitive Law did more to spread the ills of slavery in the free states and to make slavery a national issue than any event up to that time. The slavery issue also influenced the popular novel *Uncle Tom's Cabin* by abolitionist Harriet Beecher Stowe, published in 1851. The novel depicted the harsh conditions for enslaved Africans and influenced antislavery sentiments in America.

The Kansas-Nebraska Act, 1854[11]

This event lead to the US Civil War. To understand the motive for introducing the act, the political and economic interests involved, and the attempts to circumvent the US Constitution is to understand American racism.

The unorganized land in dispute was the northern part of the Louisiana Territory purchased from France in 1803. The land was commonly called Indian Territory because Native Americans had been removed from their lands east of the Mississippi River and relocated on reservations established by US government policy, Indian Removal Act of 1830: Florida, Georgia, Mississippi, Alabama, Tennessee, and North Carolina. Tribes from New York, Michigan,

---

[11]   "Kansas–Nebraska Act," Wikipedia, last modified September 15, 2008, https://en.wikipedia.org/wiki/Kansas%E2%80%93Nebraska_Act

Illinois, Iowa, and Missouri had also been relocated to reservations in this territory.

The Missouri Compromise of 1820 assured settlers who had started pouring into Nebraska without federal government permission that slavery could not be established in the territory. Under the Missouri Compromise, slavery could not be established above 36°30' latitude.

Led by railroad interests and business entrepreneurs President Franklin Pierce and US Senator Stephen A. Douglas, Democrat, Illinois, wanted to organize the territory and build a continental railroad across the territory.

Southern Slave Supporters (SSS) led by Senator David Atchison, Democrat, Missouri, staunchly opposed any expansion that banned slavery.

Senator Stephen Douglass, Democrat of Illinois, introduced a bill to organize the territories of Kansas and Nebraska that set off a fierce debate over slavery. Both were north of latitude 36°30', and therefore the Missouri Compromise prohibited slavery from consideration. Additionally, the territories were in lands that were considered to be Indian lands. The Southern Slavery Supporters (SSS) staunchly refused to consider the bill because it banned slavery. Douglas wanted the bill so much that he eventually caved into the SSS's demands to repeal the Missouri Compromise. Northern senators were incensed but feared the Democrats with the solid support of the SSS had the votes to pass the bill. Both the house and senate members of the Whig/Republican Party expressed their outrage in the hearings and relied on the voters to denounce the bill and stop its enactment.

Senator Douglas also believed that repealing the Missouri Compromise would take the slavery issue out of the judicial prerogative of Congress and allow the people in the territory to decide under the popular sovereignty concept (i.e., the people of the territory of Kansas and Nebraska would decide to enter the union as either a free or slave state). As Douglas and the Democrats desired, the bill passed, and President Pierce signed it into law on May 30, 1854. The expansion of slavery now became a national issue. Newspapers, the main public media at the time, began spreading the news from a partisan perspective. Northern papers were generally republican and southern generally democrat. The people and the government were split.

The territory of Kansas became known as Bleeding Kansas from the time the Kansas-Nebraska bill passed until 1859, when the majority of Kansas voted to enter the union as a free state. Kansas was flooded with proslavery Missourians and abolitionists and free soilers from the eastern states to persuade the people of Kansas to vote for a free or slave state. The concept of popular sovereignty turned into guerilla warfare between the proslavery Missouri Ruffians and the Kansas Jayhawkers (white farmers against competing with slave labor to earn their livelihood). Four different groups claiming to represent the people of Kansas established their own state constitution. The Wyandotte Constitution passed in 1859 was the only one confirmed to represent voters who lived in Kansas, and their vote was for a free state. The US House of Representatives passed the bill to admit Kansas as a free state immediately. Ironically, the US Senate passed the bill to approve Kansas as a free state on January 29, 1861, after eleven slave states seceded from the union, and their senators left their seats on January 21. 1861.

Abraham Lincoln, Republican, Illinois, challenged Stephen A. Douglas to represent the state of Illinois as its senator, gave a speech in October 1854 at Peoria, Illinois, that explained his views against slavery. He spoke for three hours and stated that the flaw of slavery in the US Constitution of 1778 was leading the country farther away from the beliefs proposed in the Declaration of Independence. He stated, "Little by little, but steadily as man's march to the grave, we have been giving up the old for the new faith. Nearly eighty years ago we began by declaring that all men are created equal, but now from that beginning we have run down to the other declaration, that for some men to enslave others is a 'sacred right of self-government.' These principles cannot stand together. They are as opposite as God and Mammon, and whoever holds to the one must despise the other." His clarity and passion for the belief's in the Declaration of Independence earned him prominence with the newly formed Republican Party. He was elected as the sixteenth president of the

United States and preserved the union, abolished slavery, and added the enslaved African to the mosaic of "We the People."

A Personal Perspective of Slavery and My Family Heritage: William Henry Dant—A Slave in Kentucky and Missouri

As a personal link to slavery and its generational impact, my ancestry arrived in Missouri in 1821 shortly after statehood and remained enslaved until emancipated in January 1865. William Henry Dant was my great-great grandfather and my mother's grandfather. Henry's enslavement was sanctioned under the lawful practice of human bondage in the Constitution of 1787 and the government of the United States.

Joe Dant, Henry's father, was enslaved by J. W. Dant of Kentucky Bourbon Distillery fame and sold to Daniel Kendrick in Kentucky, who brought him to Monroe County, Missouri, in 1827 just seven years after statehood. Joe would have been around seventeen years old at the time they arrived in Missouri, and we don't know how many other slaves the Kendricks brought with them. We do know that Joe had a wife and two sons. One son, William Henry Dant, my great-great grandfather, was born enslaved in Monroe County in 1835. He took a wife (details of her owner unknown) and had two children while enslaved. We don't know the birth date of daughter, Evaline, but do know that Charles Abraham Dant, my grandfather, was born in 1857. William Henry Dant and his family who had been condemned slaves for life was set free in 1865 when the state of Missouri emancipated all slaves in the state. Henry lived to the ripe old age of 105 and told his story to a member of the Federal Writers' Project (FWP), commissioned by President Franklin Roosevelt, 1936–1938. Volunteers of the FWP went around the country capturing the stories of formerly enslaved Africans.

The highlights of Henry's enslavement are about his fears performing assigned jobs during the final days of the Civil War in Ralls County. He also noted that Daniel Kendrick had been a "big man" as a judge in Ralls County in those days, and Henry had to make a lot of trips to New London, Missouri, to the county seat. For thirty years, while enslaved, Henry worked for food and shelter for himself and extended family consisting of his mother, brother, and two children. The work consisted of planting and reaping crops in season—often working from sunup to can't see, feeding and caring for livestock, herding stock to market, and running errands in between. They made baskets during winter months. Henry played a fiddle for white entertainment events and earned 15 cents that he was allowed to keep. He lamented that when freed in 1865, he was given a side of meat and a bag of meal to start life as a former enslaved black man. He was not yet a citizen of the US because the Fourteenth Amendment had not yet been passed. He worked on a farm after emancipation and was restricted by state and local laws enforcing racial segregation on the type work he was allowed to perform, location of type and quality of residence, educational opportunities, places to purchase goods and services, places of worship, and cemetery of interment.

Charlie, my grandfather, was eight years old when Henry was freed by the state of Missouri. Charlie was governed by the same restrictions as Henry and as an adult who worked on a farm and raised thirteen children. One of his children completed college and taught school in Hannibal, Missouri. The other twelve (nine girls and three boys) in their adult lives labored for others, and one owned his own farm. Most owned their homes and sacrificed to educate their children. Ten of Charlie's grandchildren (I am one of twenty-two) graduated from college and successfully navigated institutional racism to enjoy an American middle- or upper-middle-class lifestyle. A few of Charlie's grandchildren successfully worked their way out of intercity poverty and provided their children with college education and entry into the American middle class.

William Henry's legacy was thirteen children who worked hard to navigate the barriers of racism so their children could be more prosperous than themselves. They were constantly aware of racial barriers imposed by segregation and worked hard to overcome them.

The extended family of Dant-Scott-Wright-Trott continues the legacy of taking care of our own and preparing our children to do the same through education. We are blessed with our share of lawyers, engineers, executives, teachers, blue-collar workers, entrepreneurs, and a brigadier general and command sergeant major. We, too, worked hard to overcome the hardships and barriers of our enslaved ancestors and the Jim Crow restrictions imposed on us. However, our family's success does not mean that all African Americans should be able to overcome the barriers and hardships imposed on their enslaved and disenfranchised ancestors, especially those from the southern confederate states.

Many generations of Americans of African descent from the southern states desperately migrated to the northern states in massive numbers between 1915–1970 in search of jobs and freedom. Isabel Wilkerson, author of *The Warmth of Other Suns*,[12] documented how blatant and institutional racism over time dashed the hopes of hundreds of thousands and created the ghettos in America's intercities. Factories closed or relocated, job and housing discrimination, zip code discrimination, lack of health-care facilities, limited or no access to healthy food choices, and underresourced public schools are just a few of the barriers that imprison intercity residents.

The problem was created by the southern states with the complicity of the federal government. It should be resolved by the federal and state governments. Reparations or restitution for the generations of unpaid labor of our enslaved African ancestors is a possible solution. This is one of my proposals on how you can stop institutional racism.

A special note of thanks to Tim Dant for contributing information about the enslavement of William Henry Dant. Tim is the great-great grandson of J. W. Dant who owned and sold Joe Dant, William Henry's father, to the Kendricks. Tim, a sports enthusiast, saw Jenni Dant, daughter of Joel Dant, play basketball in a nationally televised DePaul University game and became curious about the name connection. Joel is also the grandson of Charles Abraham Dant, William Henry's son. Tim contacted and, subsequently with his son, visited Joel and his wife, Faye, and with me in Hannibal, Missouri, in his search for the connection between the white and black Dant families. He confirmed the slave transaction as reported

---

[12]   Isabel Wilkerson, The Warmth of Other Suns (New York: Random House, 2010).

above and learned through Ancestry.com that there was no biological connection between the two Dant families. Tim exhibits the courage and compassion required to bridge racial barriers and to put a stop to institutional racism. I have great respect for Tim, and biological connection excepted, Tim is a relative in spirit and in courage.

CHAPTER FIVE

Abraham Lincoln's New Birth of Freedom: Racist, Realist, Reformer

WHEN IN THE COURSE OF human events and men of goodwill act with rancor, disrespect, and ridicule toward those who do not share their view only the man of civility can find common ground to represent the best interest of all. Abraham Lincoln was a man of civility.

"Civility is about more than just politeness, although politeness is a necessary first step. It is about disagreeing without disrespect, seeking common ground as a starting point for dialogue about differences, listening past one's preconceptions, and teaching others to do the same. Civility is the hard work of staying present even with those with whom we have deep-rooted and fierce disagreements. It is political in the sense that it is a necessary perquisite for civic action. But it is political, too, in the sense that it is about negotiating interpersonal power such that everyone's voice is heard, and nobody's is ignored."[13]

The SSS and sympathizers were noted for their uncompromising stance on their rights to own slaves, and even President Lincoln's

---

13   "What Is Civility?" The Institute of Civility in Government, last modified June 11, 2013, www.instituteforcivility.org/who-we-are/what-is-civility.

cabinet were noted for their strong disagreements with Lincoln over policy matters.[14]

Disagreements over the issue of slavery in America divided communities, families, individuals, governments from local to federal levels, and churchgoing members of all religious denominations. And most divisive of all was the split between the professional military men who felt compelled to leave the American forces to join and defend the Confederate cause.

As president, Lincoln chose to preserve the union above all other considerations and in the course of armed conflict reaffirmed what he already knew, that the union could not be restored with slavery remaining a part of the American principle of equality. His toughest challenge was the disposition of the enslaved African.

Lincoln the Racist

During the early years of the war, the union forces were in search of a victory, and in 1862, President Lincoln was encouraging his commanders for a victory so that he could issue a proclamation to free slaves in states of the rebellion that the union controlled. At the same time, Lincoln was looking for solutions for removing enslaved Africans from America. His meeting and frank talk about enslaved Africans leaving the USA for colonization in other countries is a remarkable example of Lincoln's blunt expression of racist views while acknowledging the plight of the enslaved in America.

Early in the spring of 1862, President Lincoln had urged the congress to provide a sum of money to send enslaved Africans to be colonized in South America. His thinking was that if there were no enslaved Africans, there would be no war between the states. Assured of the appropriation, the president invited a group of free blacks to the White House to inform them of his proposition to colonize enslaved Africans (to include them) in other parts of the world and to get their support of his efforts. This was the first record of free

---

[14]   "Abraham Lincoln, Remarks on Colonization to African-American Leaders, August 14, 1862," House Divided: The Civil War Research Engine at Dickinson College, http://hd.housedivided.dickinson.edu/node/40448.

Africans in America being invited to meet with the president of the United States. His candor and approach on the sensitive subject of slavery, race, and status reveals the unique quality Lincoln possessed to separate his feelings and beliefs from those who fiercely opposed slavery from those who adamantly supported it. This was an example of Lincoln's civility at an awkward time.

On August 14, 1862, the president met with a committee of colored men at the White House and, after a preliminary observations, informed them that a sum of money had been appropriated by Congress and placed at his disposition for the purpose of aiding the colonization in some country of the people, or a portion of them, of African descent, thereby making it his duty, as it had for a long time been his inclination, to favor that cause. And "why," he asked, "should the people of your race be colonized, and where? Why should they leave this country? This is, perhaps, the first question for proper consideration. You and we are different races, We have between us a broader difference that exists between almost any other two races. Whether it is right or wrong I need not discuss, but this physical difference is a great disadvantage to us both, as I think your race suffer very greatly, any of them by living among us, while ours suffer from your presence. In a word we suffer on each side. If this is admitted, it affords a reason at least why we should be separated."

After pausing to tell them that he supposed that they were freemen, and hearing that they were indeed free, he continued with his insightful observations.

"Your race are suffering, in my judgement, the greatest wrong inflicted on any people. But even when you cease to be slaves, you are yet far removed from being placed on an equality with the white race. You are cut off from many of the advantages which the other race enjoy. The aspiration of men is to enjoy equality with the best when free, but on this broad continent, not a single man of your race is made the equal of a single man of ours. Go where you are treated the best, and the ban is still upon you. I do not propose to discuss this, but to present it as a fact with which we have to deal. I cannot alter it if I would. It is a fact, about which we all think and feel alike, I and you."

Lincoln continues to share insights about ill effects slavery has on white people of the day and his belief that the war would end if there were no slaves.

"We look to your condition, owing to the existence of the two races on this continent. I need not recount to you the effects upon white men, growing out of the institution of slavery. I believe in its general evil effects on the white race. See our present condition— the country engaged in war! Our white men cutting one another's throats, none knowing how far it will extend, and then consider what we know to be the truth. But for your race among us there could not be war, although many men engaged on either side do not care for you one way or the other. Nevertheless, I repeat, without the institution of slavery and the colored race as a basis, the war could not have an existence."

Lincoln spends a considerable portion of his time attempting to persuade the delegation of the advantages in climate, opportunity to build their own community, and to build their own economy either in Liberia or Central America. He emphasizes that just because they are free in the US, their opportunities will be limited and the racial climate will be hostile. He asks the committee to recruit 100 to 150 able bodied men with children and families to begin the experiment. He also infers that there were a group of white businessmen willing to underwrite their work in the coal mines to help establish the colony. Yet he injects some uncertainty in the reception they would receive by the local leaders and promised his best to make them the equals of their Central American neighbors.

"I shall if I get a sufficient number of you engaged, have provisions made that you shall not be wronged. If you will engage in the enterprise, I will spend some of the money entrusted to me. I am not sure you will succeed. The government may lose the money, but we cannot succeed unless we try; but we think, with care, we can succeed. The political affairs in Central America are not in quite a satisfactory condition as I wish. There are contending factions in that quarter; but it is true all of the factions are agreed alike on the subject of colonization, and want it, and are more generous than we are here. To your colored race they have no objection. Besides, I would endeavor to have you made equals, and have the best assurance that you should be the equals of the best."

The delegation promised to give the president a reply after consultation with free blacks in the cities of Philadelphia, New York, and Boston. But a week after the meeting, the free blacks in Washington hotly debated the proposal and flatly turned it down. The project came to an end when two unconnected sources reported significant obstacles to executing the plan.

President Lincoln had asked Brigadier General Butler, considered a friend of the Negro and in command of troops occupying New Orleans, to carefully calculate how many ships and seaworthy vessels it would take to move four million slaves to Central America. Butler responded after a couple of weeks of calculations that there were not enough vessels and the birth rate among four million blacks would multiply their numbers faster than new vessels could be built. Then sometimes in September 1862, the project was abandoned when first Honduras and later Nicaragua and Costa Rica protested the colonization scheme and hinted that force might be used to prevent the settlement.

Lincoln the Realist

President Lincoln, the realist, accepted the facts and reexamined his options for dealing with the slaves and ending the rebellion to reunite the union. While the president was negotiating colonization of all slaves, he reluctantly authorized the recruitment of blacks to serve in union forces in July 1862. He, unbeknown to his cabinet, had worked on a proclamation to free the slaves in rebellion states and was waiting for a union victory before announcing the measure. Shortly after the union victory at Antietam in September 1862, Lincoln issued his proclamation freeing the slaves in the states of the rebellion. The purpose of the war had now escalated from restoring the union only to now restoring the union and freeing the slaves. He would leave no doubt in the minds of northern citizens or confederate rebels that his goal was to restore America to her original purpose without the sanctions allowing slavery to exist in the United States

Constitution. His Gettysburg speech in November 19, 1863, four months after the deadliest battle that claimed fifty thousand killed, wounded, or missing on both sides left no doubt that he now viewed the struggle between the states as a new birth of freedom for a united America without slavery.

The president used only 217 words and about two minutes to say that the union soldiers died to end slavery and create the America the founding fathers envisioned in the Declaration of Independence in 1776. Lincoln cleverly stated that eighty-seven years ago, America's founders declared that all men were created equal and that the Civil War was testing whether the nation or any nation so conceived and so dedicated can long endure. America would endure because her president, Abraham Lincoln, had the rare ability to examine the white supremacist attitude and racial bias of most white citizens and accept the wisdom that still escapes their posterity; the enslaved Africans and their descendants are an integral part of America's identity. The founding fathers inherently knew that to be true in 1776 but operated against that principle for eighty-seven years. It took the Civil War and Abraham Lincoln to recognize that fact and guide the nation to its founding purpose. To reach that conclusion required a combination of intellect, instinct, impulse, and divine thoughts. I believe Lincoln to have been blessed with an abundance of those qualities in the midst of the staggering life and death situations no other American president has had to confront. Those qualities enabled him to become a reformer.

Lincoln the Reformer

After Gettysburg and during the last eighteen months of his life, Lincoln increasingly introduced measures to reunite the country and accept an America without slaves.

Amnesty for Secessionist

In December 1863, one month after his Gettysburg address, Lincoln turned his attention to drafting a proclamation of amnesty for white southerners. He used his legal skills to dissect the southern political class as a means to rapidly rebuild a government structure that would be fair to all citizens of the south. Lincoln divided the white southern population by the landowner class and figured that if he could get 10 percent of that class in each state that rebelled to sign an oath of loyalty to the United States of America, the states could rapidly form state governments and grant all the rights of citizenship to their people. The other mandate for reentry was for the loyal class to implement civil rights laws to help the Negro, whom he labeled the "laboring, landless, and homeless class," out of property. Although the Thirteenth Amendment to abolish slavery would not be passed until January 31, 1865, Lincoln expected that it would become the law of the land and that all the southern states would have to ratify it to regain entry into the union. His assassination would nullify his influence over reconstruction and helping the "laboring, landless, and homeless class" get out of poverty and become citizens with status. His second inaugural address,[15] given forty-one days before he was assassinated, was designed to instruct, encourage, and explain to Americans how and why the war started and on what they needed to do to heal the country without the corrosive effects of slavery.

The Cause of the War

"One eight of the whole population were colored slaves, not distributed generally over the Union, but located in the Southern part of it. These slaves constituted a peculiar and powerful interest. All knew that this interest was somehow, the cause of the war. To strengthen, perpetuate, and extend this interest was the object for which the insurgents would rend the Union, even by war; while the government claimed no right to do more than to restrict the territorial enlargement of it. Neither party expected for the war, the magnitude, or the duration, which it has already attained. Neither anticipated that the cause of the conflict might cease, or even before

---

[15]   Ronald C. White Jr., *Lincoln's Greatest Speech* (New York: Simon & Schuster, 2002) 13–19.

the conflict itself should cease. Each looked for an easier triumph, and a result less fundamental and astounding."

This last paragraph of his address also showed Lincoln, the reformer, boldly telling the world that the American government would continue to be strong enough to forgive and help all who committed offenses against each other and at the same time remain at peace with all nations.

"With malice toward none; with charity for all; with firmness in the right, as God gives us to see the right, let us strive on to finish the work we are in; to bind up the nation's wounds; to care for him who shall have borne the battle, and for his widow, and his orphan—to do all which may achieve and cherish a just, and a lasting peace, among ourselves, and with all nations."

President Lincoln, born in a racism-practicing country, died believing that the black race was not equivalent to the white race but that they were created by God and deserved the opportunity to earn the right to live by the sweat of their own work. His courage to admit that the four million African slaves were landless, homeless, and disenfranchised and needed help from the government to remedy their condition placed him in the minority of his white fellow citizens. His all-out push to pass the Thirteenth Amendment to the Constitution to abolish slavery also undergirds his label as a realist; he knew that white southerners with the apathy of most whites in the country would seek to expand slavery to every state in the union if the three-fifths clause remained in the Constitution. For his unswerving commitment to the belief that all men are created equal by their creator as promised in the Declaration of Independence, Abraham Lincoln must always be the patron saint of American democracy. He ensured the legal removal of shackles from enslaved Africans and paved the way for them to join the portrait as African Americans and be included in the portrait of "We the People"—although legally free African Americans would still be disenfranchised by state governments for another eighty-five years and be excluded in the portrait of "We the People."

PART III

Erasing the American Stain of White Supremacy

H ARD TRUTH NUMBER 3: AMERICAN norms have always
been established by the majority white race in all forms
of human endeavor. The legal abolishment of slavery in
1865 was immediately replaced by the adoption of legal measures
to disenfranchise Negroes and people of color: the Black Codes, Jim
Crow,[16] and Separate but Equal laws enforced by the southern states
to keep Negroes separate from whites, their work opportunities were
restricted to low-paying jobs on farms or in factories, and their learning and living opportunities restricted to low-income areas segregated
by race. The Black Codes, Jim Crow, Separate but Equal, all became
white norms for controlling former slaves in the south and border
states. Northern white Americans, mostly apathetic over the treatment of blacks in the south, somehow adopted the separation of the
races in the cities and supported racial segregation in social events.

The point of this truth is that white Americans have through
manipulation and population density always been the majority race
and in positions to enforce institutional racism to protect their interest or privilege. Historically, the slave-holding southern states bonded
to keep blacks and people of color from exercising equal freedoms,

---

16   "Jim Crow laws," Wikipedia, last modified March 3, 2016, https://en.wiki-
      pedia.org/wiki/Jim_Crow_laws.

justice, and citizenship. Institutional racism is deeply embedded in the American culture and governance. Issues of race and the collective racial bias of elected and appointed officials keep the American governance system favoring the white majority. Think of America as a three-legged stool.

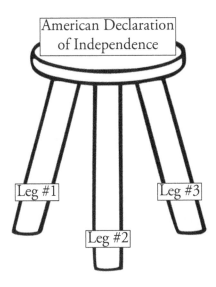

The Seat: represents America and the proposition that all men are created equal and endowed by their creator with the right to life, liberty, and the pursuit of happiness

Leg #1: the people of all races, cultures, and beliefs

Leg #2: the Constitution and three branches of government

Leg #3: individuals elected, appointed, and sworn to enforce the laws and equal rights of each American, regardless of race, gender, or national origin

In 243 years, legs numbers 2 and 3 have been wobbly because of manipulated flaws to enforce institutional racism to disenfranchise African Americans, people of color, and women. In times of national crisis, Civil War, WWI and WWII, and the Depression, the hopes of the disenfranchised inspired them to do their best so they could receive equal treatment and enjoy the rights guaranteed every

American citizen. Five presidents have attacked racism that favored their generation and ancestors to correct the flaws that weakened America's founding principles. Direct influencers were a NAACP civil rights lawyer and chief justice of the US Supreme Court. The greatness of America is her never-ending struggle to provide equal rights and privileges to all of her citizens. The beacon of American identity is to allow every citizen to be as successful as they can be without disenfranchising the rights of others. The key to the American system is having elected and appointed leaders committed to the Constitution to prevent groups or entities from disenfranchising individuals on the basis of race, religion, gender, or national origin.

The only good reason to read about the past racist codes and terrorist practices in the southern and border states against African Americans is to discover the source of white supremacy / institutional racism and stop it. The history also reveals that apathy among non-targeted citizens is a wink and a nod in support of racism. American apathy with all forms of racism must also stop. It is not becoming to our founding principles. The proposition that all men are created equal and endowed by their Creator with the unalienable rights of life, liberty, and the pursuit of happiness is either a naive expression of faith or a diabolical expression of fear. The proposition is undeniably true. The five presidents and two supreme court jurists pictured on the front cover of this book tilt our experiment with democracy in favor of the undeniable truth.

CHAPTER SIX

Harry Truman: From Racist to Reformer
Thirty-Fourth President of the United States of America
May 8, 1884, Lamar, Missouri, December 26, 1972

C HANGE IS ALWAYS UNSETTLING. LINCOLN's proclamation freeing the slaves in the southern states was the most visible sign of change to the southern slave holder after the Civil War. He could see the destruction war caused to his physical property and witness his species of property walking away to freedom. Eighty-seven years of white supremacy left the slave owner without labor to rebuild, money to repair, and authority to either form his own government or participate in the union on equal terms. The strongest bond the defeated south had with the union was the white racial identity between the north and the south. Whiteness was the bond. The union's victory secured the constitution and pardoned all but a few of the top confederates and immediately began rebuilding America under what Abraham Lincoln called a new birth of freedom. The bond of white supremacy dominated reconstruction / American identity from the end of the Civil War until Harry Truman became president in 1946. Sixteen presidents of the United States would preside over the domestic rise of violence against African Americans and the exclusion of civil rights to African Americans. The most egregious un-American acts of terror and brutality were the enactment of the Black Codes, the restrictions on the freedoms of blacks to include restrictions on voting, and Jim Crow laws, the legalized separation of the races in public accommodations (i.e., separate but equal laws that resulted in a black and white America). Even the United States military were divided into all black units in the army, navy, marines and coast guard. Returning black service members from WWI and WWII were treated with disrespect, terrorized, hung, and murdered for perceptions of violating white expectations of black behavior. Over 3,600 black American lynchings were recorded in the south from 1866 to 1962. The bond among supporters of white supremacy determined election results for local, state, and federal office holders in the southern states. That bond would prove stronger than the founding principle of the nation's belief in the proposition that all men were created equal.

The southern states would resurrect white supremacy over blacks in the south with the complicity of the victorious north. The south erected statues of their generals who denounced their oath to support and defend the United States Constitution to fight against the Union Army. The American people and the United States government under sixteen US presidents after the Civil War would allow the stains on America's founding principles to flourish until Harry Truman used the power of the presidency to say enough was enough to stop the assault against African Americans and to guarantee freedom and equality for all Americans.

Harry Truman: Racist

I like Harry Truman. He was two years older than my dad, we both are from Missouri, we both identified with the prevailing racial prejudices of our era, but he was a racist until 1946. Truman grew up in Jackson County, Missouri, and proudly identified with the Confederate cause both his grandparents supported in the Civil War. He managed to get himself a commission in the US Army reserves as a first lieutenant of artillery in WWI and served in France. He proved to be a tough taskmaster in the military and met the nephew of Tom Pendergast, the political boss of Kansas City and Jackson

County, Missouri. The Pendergast connection served him well when he returned to civilian life in Kansas City, and he progressed from local judgeship appointments to become a United States senator. Pendergast supported the separate but equal mob activities in the white and black districts in Kansas City, and Truman appealed for white and black votes to win his elections. Truman was considered to be a fair man by black people of that era. In my dad's generation, a white man crowned a "fair man" could receive no higher recognition; it meant you were judged by character and reputation and not color and racial bias in business. Harry Truman carried that distinction to Washington, DC, as a US senator and earned a reputation that lead to his selection by President Franklin Roosevelt to run as his vice president.

Shortly after winning his fourth term, President Roosevelt died in April 1945, thrusting Truman in as president to preside over the US victory in Europe and to guide the war against Japan. Truman had no previous briefings from Roosevelt or from the president's cabinet on the war in either theatre. He authorized the use of the atomic bomb to end the war in Japan and approved the Marshall Plan to rebuild Europe. On the domestic front, Americans were adjusting to peace, victorious service members were returning home, and Truman was developing programs that would define his administration for the rest of Roosevelt's term. The southern states' terror against African Americans would demand a response from his administration and preempt his planning.

Southern politicians, law enforcement officials, and court justices formed a tight alliance to rigidly enforce Jim Crow and separate but equal laws against African Americans. The NAACP represented by their legal attorney, Thurgood Marshall, was busy defending black victims of Jim Crow laws and challenging separate but equal laws in school districts throughout the south.

White Mob Violence against Blacks in the South

In the early months of 1946, two major racial incidents occurred that provoked white defense of killing blacks and the NAACP requesting Truman to demand the whites responsible for the killings be prosecuted. The events in February 1946 in Columbia, Tennessee, began with an argument over the repair of a radio owned by a black woman accompanied by her navy veteran son with a white clerk, son of the store owner. The black woman and the clerk argued over the repair order, the clerk aggressively threatened her, and her son intervened. The clerk crashed through the department store window, the police were called, and the woman and her son were charged with disturbing the peace and paid a $50 dollar fine. Later that day, the store owner filed a warrant for the son's arrest, and he was charged with assault and intent to commit murder, a felony. A black business-man posted the bond, and the son was allowed to go home. The end of the incident?

That night, a white mob gathered around the Maury County Courthouse. A block south of the courthouse was the black business part of town called Mink Slide, and black citizens that included black veterans also assembled. The Columbia police chief sent four police-men to Mink Slide, and someone in the crowd yelled for them to stop. When they didn't, shots were fired wounding all four. Within hours, the state safety commissioner, state highway patrol men, and a group of white citizens poised to enter Mink Slide. The highway patrol went in first, shot up the buildings, stole goods, cash, and searched homes without warrants. They took pistols, shotguns, rifles, and arrested about one hundreds blacks who were held without bail and denied legal counsel. The Columbia "riot" made headlines in northern newspapers and caught Truman's attention. But the worse was not over. Two days later, on February 28, the Columbia police-men killed two black prisoners in custody and wounded a third pris-oner. The police claimed that the officers were interrogating the pris-oners when they attempted to grab the officers' guns. Walter White, president, NAACP, and Thurgood Marshall, NAACP legal counsel, went to Tennessee to represent the black prisoners and were harassed by law enforcement until they left the state. President Truman was informed of this incident, but several other violent acts against blacks would occur in the south before July 1946 that would greatly impact Truman's involvement with civil rights.

In Walton County, Georgia, on the afternoon of July 25, 1946, four African Americans were pulled from a car by a white mob, "beaten, tortured and fatally shot. Their skulls were cracked, their flesh was torn, and their limbs were shredded." George Dorsey, a distinguished World War II veteran, and Roger Malcolm were share croppers on land owned by J. Loy Harrison. Two weeks before the lynching, Roger Malcolm had been arrested and charged with stabbing a white farmer during a fight. Two weeks after the fight, J. Loy Harrison drove Mrs. Malcolm and the Dorseys to the jail to post a $600 bond for Malcolm's release. On the way back to the farm, the car was stopped by a mob of thirty armed, unmasked white men who seized Malcolm and Dorsey and tied them to a large oak tree." Dorothy Malcolm recognized some of the men in the mob. "When she called on them by name to spare her husband," according to the FBI report, "the mob seized her and Mrs. Dorsey... The white land owner watched as the white mob fatally shot the couples...near the Moore's Ford wooden bridge over the Apalachee River."[17] President Truman was informed of this violent crime and directed the Justice Department to investigate it.

By July 1946, Sgt. Isaac Woodard's blinding was gaining wide publicity, and the National Association of Colored Women's Club picketed the White House carrying signs that read "Speak Mr. President Speak." During the same time frame, the NAACP organized an umbrella group of about forty civil rights organizations, the National Emergency Committee against Mob Violence, and requested a meeting with President Truman on September 19.

The blinding of Sgt. Isaac Woodard took place on February 12, 1946, in Batesburg, South Carolina. Woodard had his eyes gouged out by the chief of police in Batesburg, South Carolina. He had been honorably discharged from the US Army, still in uniform, and on his way home to North Carolina. He boarded the bus in Georgia and at a stop near Augusta, South Carolina, asked the bus driver if he could

---

17   DeNeen L. Brown, "Appeals court orders grand jury testimony unsealed in the 1946 case of the 'Last Mass Lynching in America,'" *The Washington Post*, February 12, 2019, https://www.washingtonpost.com/history/2019/02/12/appeals-court-orders-grand-jury-testimony-unsealed-case-last-mass-lynching-america.

get off to relieve himself. The driver profanely told him to go back to his seat. Woodard demanded that he be treated and spoken to like a man and went back to his seat. At the next town of Batesburg, the bus driver stopped at the police station and reported that Woodard was drinking and causing problems. The policeman, Linwood Shull, took Woodard off the bus and hit him over the head with his billy club because Woodard's answer didn't please him. Once inside the police station, Shull hit Woodard with the club and Woodard wrestled the club from him. A second policeman entered the station at that moment, pulled his pistol on Woodard, and ordered him to drop the club. Shull picked up the club and started beating Woodard over the head until he was unconscious. Shull then used the end of the club to gouge both eyes out and left Woodard in the jail cell until the next morning.

Woodard's eyes were swollen and dried blood on his face and head when Shull awakened him to take him to the judge for sentencing. Shull had to help clean the blood and help Woodard navigate since his vision was blurred. Shull took Woodard to the judge who sentenced him for being drunk and disorderly and fined him $50 or thirty days hard labor on the chain gain. Woodard searched his pockets and found only $44 dollars, which the judge accepted. Woodard's injuries and loss of sight prevented him from moving about without assistance, so Shull took Woodard to the VA in Columbia, South Carolina. The VA didn't have an eye specialist on staff but retained him for treatment and observation. The VA released the blinded Woodard to a cousin who helped him get to New York where his family had moved to escape southern white brutality. Woodard's wife deserted him, and his only income was a $50 monthly disability check from the VA. The NAACP sponsored a fundraiser to publicize violence against blacks in the south. Some of the proceeds were used to purchase a home for Woodard and to take him on a tour to publicize the brutal attack that blinded him. The Sgt. Isaac Woodard tour was gaining wide publicity by the September 1946 meeting with President Truman and the National Emergency Committee against Mob Violence (NECAMV) convened at the White House.

NAACP and Civil Rights Groups Petition Truman to Stop the Violence

Walter White, NAACP president and respected by President Truman, was the apparent leader of the coalition of the civil rights NECAMV umbrella group. The consensus of the group was that the Justice Department investigations of recent mob violence against blacks in the south produced no indictments. Spokespersons were unanimous in their appeals for the president to do something to stop the violence. They proposed that he call the Congress into special session to adopt federal anti-lynching legislation. Truman listened sympathetically and told them "Everyone seems to believe the president by himself can do anything he wishes to on such matters as this. But the president is helpless unless he is backed by public opinion" (p. 72). Walter White perceived that the president didn't understand the brutality behind the murders and begin describing the details of how the Batesburg Chief of Police blinded Sgt. Isaac Woodard. As the story unfolded, Truman sat riveted and became visibly agitated and angered. One observer later described his face as "distorted in horror." Casting his staff's advice aside, and obviously distressed president responded, "My God! I had no idea it was as terrible as that! We have got to do something" (p. 73). Truman appoints the first President's Committee on Civil Rights and charges them to present recommendations that will end the violence. From that moment of awareness and awakening, President Truman acted as a man whose obligation to his Creator and oath to the US Constitution took priority over his loyalty to his confederate heritage, white supremacy, and institutional racism. His civil rights initiatives moved America closer to the founding beliefs in the Declaration of Independence.

Truman Energizes Justice Department That Sends Message to the South That Enough Is Enough

President Truman's letter to Tom Clark, attorney general, set off a series of actions that reverberated throughout the south. Truman specifically told Clark about "the negro sergeant" and his "eyes being deliberatively put out" and that it was time to do something about it. The next day, September 25, 1946, the Civil Rights Section of the Justice Department issued criminal charges against Lynwood Shull, chief of police of Batesburg, South Carolina, for blinding Sgt. Isaac Woodard. To be sure the charges were carried out promptly and precisely, Turner Smith, chief of the Civil Rights Section, called Claud Sapp, US attorney for South Carolina District. Smith told Sapp to file criminal charges against Shull as a misdemeanor with max punishment of one year; that charge would avoid a time-consuming federal grand jury and their option to dismiss the charge. Sapp knew that the southern law enforcement alliance would push back against the federal government meddling in the state's rights and planned to file as instructed but use his option to dismiss after filing. But outmaneuvering Sapp, the Justice Department released the statement before calling Sapp that read, "Criminal charges have been filed against Lynwood Lanier Shull, Bates Burg, SC Chief of Police, for violating the right of Isaac Woodward Jr., not to be beaten and tortured by persons exercising the authority to arrest." The public announcement by the US Attorney General alarmed southern politicians, judges, and law enforcement officials—they colluded to undermine the prosecution against Shull.

The FBI agents from the Savannah district were directed to provide their files to Sapp. They expressed their concerns about the charges by the Justice Department jeopardizing their working relationship with southern law enforcement officials. One of the agents sent a personal correspondence to J. Edgar Hoover, director of the FBI. Local sheriffs, US senators from the south, and even some district judges were angry over the Justice Department's prosecution of what they considered the state's responsibility to handle their internal affairs. Judge Timmerman of District of Columbia, South Carolina, where the trial would be held, recused himself because of his dislike of federal prosecutors meddling in his jurisdiction. He asked District Judge Waties Waring, Charleston, to preside over the trial. Waring, a son of the south and upholder of the Jim Crow laws, presided over the trial on November 4, 1946. He was a changed man after the verdict was announced against Shull.

Claud Sapp, prosecutor against Shull, usually an effective lawyer in the court room, appeared ill prepared. Medical records were not subpoenaed from the VA, and two witness that saw Shull hit Woodard over the head with his club were not called. And the most flagrant omission of all was Sapp's closing argument, telling the jurors that the government would be satisfied with whatever decision they delivered. They delivered a unanimous not guilty verdict for Shull.

Truman was disappointed but not deterred in his efforts to stop the evil of the mob violence. Judge Waring and his wife were devastated. He was committed to the rule of law and became an ally with President Truman, Thurgood Marshall, Walter White, and many in the civil rights community. Waring was a key strategist in the fight to overturn *Plessy v. Ferguson*, the southern white supremacist's legal justification to keep the white and black races separated.

Truman's Contribution to the Declaration of Independence and the Constitution

President Truman used the power of his office and his effective persuasion abilities to influence the leaders of his Democratic Party to support and enact civil rights laws that would guarantee all Americans equal rights under the constitution. The southern democrats adamantly opposed Truman. They were so angry with Truman's support of civil rights, they bolted the party and formed a third party, the Dixie Democrats, under Strom Thurmond, South Carolina, for president. President Truman used his office and executive authority to correct institutional racism embedded in the constitution since its creation in 1778. His historic accomplishments are underappreciated and not given deserved credit for moving America away from the stains of white supremacy and toward the superpower and champion of freedom and justice for all Americans. His impressive accomplishments began with the following:

The First President to Speak Before the NAACP

On June 29, 1947, at the base of the Lincoln Memorial, President Truman delivered a twelve-minute inspirational speech before an audience of thousands present and millions listening over four radio networks. His most informative excerpt from the speech conveyed his commitment to securing the rights of all Americans and its importance to the country's birthright. He declared that "our immediate task is to remove the last remnants of the barriers that stand between millions of our citizens and their birthright." He maintained there was "no justifiable reason for discrimination because of ancestry, or religion, or race, or color." He asserted that the rights of American citizenship included the right to a decent home, a quality education, adequate medical care, a worthwhile job, equal access to the ballot, and a fair trial in a fair court. He addressed the recent incidents of mob violence and emphasized that the country had not yet "secured to each citizen full freedom from fear." He noted the urgency of the need to remedy these evils now and not wait another generation. He concluded by expressing confidence that while the way ahead is not easy, we can reach the goal (with skillful and vigorous action). Referring to the principles of the Declaration of Independence, the US Constitution, the Emancipation Proclamation, and the proposed United Nations International Bill of Rights, he concluded that "with these noble charters to guide us...we shall make our land a happier home for our people, a symbol of hope for all men, and a rock of security in a troubled world."

Acceptance of Report of President's Committee on Civil Rights: Comprehensive Listing of Policies, Practices within the Federal Government that Promote American Racism

The committee consisted of sixteen racially and gender diverse Americans. They were from the north as well as the south, corporate executives, educators, union members, and clergy. The committee was convened in December 1946 and disbanded in December 1947. The report was titled "To Secure these Rights": "the right to safety and security of the person," "the right to citizenship and its privileges," "the right to freedom of conscience and expression," and "the right to equality of opportunity." Their recommendations to secure these rights were considered radical for the times. The most radical was to abolish racial segregation in the American Armed Service, abolish racial segregation in the federal government, and that the "entire scheme of disenfranchisement and government-mandated racial segregation was grounded upon legal doctrines explicitly sanctioned by the US Supreme Court, despite the provisions of the Thirteenth, Fourteenth, and Fifteenth Amendments requiring the elimination of the last vestiges of slavery, the equal protection of the laws, and the right to vote for all citizens."

February 1948, President Truman sent the first special message to Congress to deal specifically with civil rights. He wrote congress that his first goal "is to secure fully our essential human rights. I am now presenting to the Congress my recommendations for legislation to carry us forward toward that goal... We shall not however, finally achieve the ideals for which this Nation was founded so long as any American suffers discrimination as a result of his race, religion, or color, or the land of origin of his forefathers... We cannot be satisfied until all our people have equal opportunities for jobs, for homes, for education, for health, and for political expression, and until all our people have equal protection under the law." Truman was running for reelection, and a Gallup poll indicated that the majority of Americans opposed his civil rights proposals. And especially the southern democrats who formed their own party to oppose him in the presidential election.

July 26,1948, President Truman issued Executive Orders 9981 to desegregate the Armed Forces and Executive Order 9980 that prohibited discrimination in federal employment.

Eleven days before announcing the executive orders, the Democratic Party was having its convention in Philadelphia, and the southern democrats objected to his civil rights program and walked out of the convention. They formed the Dixie Crats, an independent political party, and selected Governor Strom Thurmond, South Carolina, for president. Roosevelt's former vice president before

Truman, Henry Wallace, also formed an independent political party to run against Truman. All threatened Truman's reelection and would favor Thomas E. Dewy, the Republican's presidential nominee.

The last night of the convention, Truman gave a feisty speech at the Democratic convention by deriding the "do nothing" Republicans who held the US Congress. He pointed out their failure to pass any legislation to help curb the ills of the domestic economy and blasted their record on civil rights. Truman seized the moment to excite his party and announced at the convention that he was going to call the Republicans back into a special session of Congress to pass the policies and programs they had endorsed in the Republican platform. He chose the date of July 26 for their return to Congress and also picked that date to sign Executive Orders 9981 and 9980. On the opening of the recall session, the republicans were surprised to learn of the executive orders and the country was shocked that Truman would make such a radical decision to desegregate the two largest and most powerful institutions in the federal government and especially during an election year. White citizens of neither party supported racial integration.

The polls and pundits were sure that Dewey would defeat Truman, but he took advantage of the momentum gained from attacking the "do nothing" Republicans and made a whistle stop tour through the Midwest and west to end his campaign tour. Large and energetic crowds gathered at every train stop Truman made and enthusiastically cheered "giv'em hell, Harry." He went to Harlem, New York, after the train tour and was the first US president to visit the predominantly black community—the crowd was large and enthusiastic. On the eve of the election results, the night of November 2, 1948, Truman lead Dewy in the popular vote, but polls and pundits continued to predict his defeat. The next morning, the whole world was shocked to learn that Truman defeated Dewey by a comfortable margin of electoral and popular votes. A massive number of African Americans voted for Truman in the large cities and urban areas. Truman even won eight of the eleven southern states despite the unpopularity of his stance on civil rights. As the thirty-third president of the United States, he did not waiver from his decision to desegregate the armed forces.

In early 1949, just months after signing the order to racially integrate the armed forces, President Truman dismissed the objections of four four-star army generals to desegregate the army. The first attempt to avoid integration of the army was made by Army Chief of Staff General Omar Bradley, who interpreted the language in Executive Order 9981 to mean "equal opportunity and equal treatment" in the armed forces because the word *integration* was not used. When interviewed by a reporter for clarification of the order, Bradley bluntly stated that the army was no place for social experiment and that the army would integrate when the rest of America integrated. Truman read the statement and summoned Bradley to his office for a dressing down. He made certain his intent and meaning of the desegregation order was clear. Bradley called a press conference, publicly apologized for his misstatement, and assured the public that the orders of the commander in chief would be implemented. However, the Secretary of the Army, Kenneth Royall, continued to disagree with the order and solicited the support of Generals Marshall, Eisenhower, and Mark Clark to state that army readiness would be eroded. President Truman dismissed their concerns as nonsense and appointed a racially diverse presidential committee to approve each service's implementation plan. The Air Force and Navy (Marine Corps included) approved within months. The army developed several approaches to keep blacks from totally integrating; allowing blacks serve in manual labor and supply jobs—that failed; establishing a percentage that blacks could not exceed—that failed. Secretary Royall was forced to resign, and the army plan to totally integrate was approved. Racial integration began slowly on military bases throughout the United States and American installations throughout the world. The Korean War saw the first racially integrated units use of military forces. Racial bias continued to exist within the military, but the experience helped change America; service members brought their multiracial experience from the military when they returned to civilian life.

When President Truman's stewardship of America's domestic and foreign policy ended, historians did not rank his time in office very high. He is now regarded in the top 10 of all presidents. Historians always list his greatest accomplishments as being in the international arena: dropping the atomic bomb on Japan to end the war in Asia, presiding over the Marshall Plan to rebuild Western Europe, conducting the Berlin Airlift to support the East Germany's resistance against the Russians, and for creating NATO. His civil rights accomplishments improved domestic tranquility among America's racially diverse population and raised our image among the nations of the world. His embrace in the belief in the Declaration of Independence about all people being created equal and decision to firmly oppose the practice of white supremacy was surprising to all who knew him. Two authors who dug deep into Truman's background document the brutal blinding of Sgt. Isaac Woodard as the change agent against white supremacy. *Unexampled Courage* by Richard Gergel[18] and *Truman* by David McCullough are convincing proof. While Woodard's blinding may have been the triggering event, I believe Truman's reliance on biblical teachings informed his moral behavior toward others. In that regard, I believe Truman and Abraham Lincoln made moral choices informed by their understanding of the desires of mankind by a common Creator. Truman's executive orders and example moved America closer to becoming the nation the founding fathers envisioned.

---

[18]   Richard Gergel, *Unexampled Courage* (New York: Sarah Crichton Books, 2019). 9, 115, 135–200.

CHAPTER SEVEN

The Change Agents: Marshall, Warren, Eisenhower, Kennedy and Johnson

ONCE UPON A TIME IN America, the US Constitution supported the separation of white and black people in public facilities as long as the facilities were equal. In 1893, the state of Louisiana passed a law to segregate black and white citizens in public places. Homer Plessy was seven-eighth white and tested the law by sitting in the white section of a street car and was sentenced to one year in jail for violating that law by Judge John A. Ferguson. Plessy appealed and the US Supreme Court heard the case in 1896 and ruled in favor of Ferguson. The ruling specified that as long as the facility for colored is equal to the white facility, the state is in compliance with the US Constitution. The ruling became the law of the land and was legally enforced in the southern and border states. Black school facilities were never equal and always poorly resourced. Public schools, public transportation facilities and conveyances, public parks, and drinking fountains were also included under the separate but equal doctrine. Private owners of stores, restaurants, and gas stations had the right to deny service to black people, and many exercised that right. I attended black schools and was bussed seventy miles round trip to attend a black school through my junior year. In 1954, the fruits of the NAACP and Thurgood Marshall's long fought court battles reached the Supreme Court and changed black lives in the south and border states of America. The Supreme Court Decision of 1954 declared separate but equal schools unconstitutional and forced public schools to integrate. To many white southerners, the separate but equal doctrine was the last legal barrier to the maintenance of white supremacy. The victory is a tribute to black and white Americans working together to realize the goal of the Declaration of Independence.

Thurgood Marshal (July 2, 1908–January 24, 1993) dedicated his life to the dismantling of national laws that disenfranchised African American and minorities of equal justice under the US Constitution. He is the first African American to be appointed as Solicitor General of the US Supreme Court and later as Associate Justice of the US Supreme Court.

Marshall's upbringing in a middle-class black family in Baltimore, Maryland, and his above average intellect uniquely prepared him to challenge racism in the hostile environs of the segregated south as well as in the hallowed chambers of the Supreme Court of the United States. His father taught him how to argue and support his position.[19] The young Thurgood could represent himself well in the alleys in Baltimore or in the classrooms at Lincoln and Howard. He graduated at the top of his class at Lincoln University, Pennsylvania, and at Howard University law school. He became the mentee of Charles Hamilton Houston, the dean of Howard's law school, and after graduation from law school took a position with the National Association for the Advancement of Colored People (NAACP). Thurgood used his prodigious skills to overturn discriminatory laws against African Americans as the legal counsel and president of the NAACP's Legal Defense Fund. The late Dr. John Hope Franklin, historian and former professor of Duke University, spoke of Marshall's legacy in *Ebony* magazine that puts his accomplishments in perspective:

---

[19]   Juan Williams, *Thurgood Marshall: American Revolutionary* (New York: Times Books, 1998).

> If you study the history of Marshall's career, the history of his rulings on the Supreme Court, even his dissents, you will understand that when he speaks, he is not speaking just for black Americans but for Americans of all times. He reminds us constantly of the great promise this country has made of equality, and he reminds us that it has not been fulfilled. Through his life he has been a great watchdog, insisting that this nation live up to the Constitution. (*Ebony* 45, no. 7, May 1990, p. 68).

Marshall won twenty-nine out of thirty-two Supreme Court cases as legal director for the NAACP from 1940–1961 and knocked down racially restrictive barriers established during the Jim Crow era through the separate but equal laws that restricted educational, voting, and economic rights of African Americans and other minorities. His principal strategy was to show that separate and equal schools were a violation of the Fourteenth Amendment equal protection clause to the Constitution. Between 1951–1954, under the direction of the NAACP and Thurgood Marshall, five black schools in the states of Delaware, Kansas, DC, South Carolina, and Virginia filed court cases against their state's separate and unequal schools for black students. All were argued on the basis of the comparison of black and white facilities and teacher resources. All except the South Carolina case was resolved, leaving the separate but equal standard the only measurement of equality between black and white student education. Marshall's strategy in *Briggs v. Elliott*, South Carolina, May 28, 1951, established the drama, high stakes, and influence of Judge J. Waites Waring, who shaped his argument to secure the landmark victory in *Brown v. Board of Education, Topeka*.

With the assistance of the local NAACP, the community of Summerton, South Carolina—75 percent African American—filed a case against the state of South Carolina and their school board for unequal facilities and lack of bus transportation for students in Clarendon School District Number 22. Thurgood Marshall and his team were eager to argue the case on behalf of Harry and Eliza

Briggs, lead complainants. Marshall saw the case as representative of the inequality of black schools in the Deep South and potentially more dangerous to the plaintiffs in bringing charges before the state. Judge J. Waites Waring, US District Court for Eastern District of South Carolina, was also looking for a case on his docket to end racial segregation in public schools. Waring, who had presided over the trial of Sgt. Isaac Woodard, was sickened by the travesty of justice that acquitted the chief of police who purposefully blinded Woodard and evolved to become a champion of equal rights. He and his wife had been shunned by the Charleston elite because of their outspoken stance against racism and support of black equality. The Warings had become friends with the Walter White, president of the NAACP, and members of prominent civil rights supporters. Waring had privately developed a strategy to expand the measurement of separate but equal and wanted a case that challenged the constitutionality of Plessy in front of the Supreme Court. Had a straight forward case on his docket that challenged equality of facilities and arranged a preconference with Marshall to persuade him to make a frontal attack on the constitutionality of separate but equal under Plessy in the Briggs case.

Marshall was not enthusiastic arguing that separate but equal was unconstitutional only on the basis of the equal protection clause of the Fourteenth Amendment. He considered it a high risk of failure without the concrete comparisons of black and white school facilities. Waring pushed back by explaining how his approach would guarantee the case would be heard before the Supreme Court. He explained that any case that challenged the constitutionality of a state's performance required a three-panel judge to decide the merits and any case with a dissenting vote automatically went before the Supreme Court. He was pretty certain that he would be on the panel and knew the other two judges likely to be on the panel and their likely positions in support of Plessy. Marshall felt that he did not have a better option and agreed to the approach. Waring also persuaded Marshall to refile the petition with a frontal assault against the constitutionality of Plessy. Marshall agreed and sent his assistant to meet with the plaintiffs and explain the change and advise of the likely risk of intimidation by whites in their community. The plaintiffs were steadfast in their resolve and enthusiastically supported the approach to end segregated schools. Waring completed all the documents to dismiss the original complaint without prejudice, refile the frontal assault, and establish the three-panel judge to hear the case. The historic behind the scenes maneuvers and overflow attendance by black Summerton and interested South Carolinians was in full evidence at the start of the trial on May 28, 1951.

The three-judge panel consisted of John J. Parker, chief judge, Fourth District, US District Judge George Bell Timmerman Sr., and J. Waites Waring. The crowd of black folk filled the court room with the twenty plaintiffs seated in front and outside the court house extended as far as the eye could see. Parker gaveled the trial to begin, and before he could ask Marshall to make the customary opening statement for the plaintiffs, Robert Figg, attorney for the school board, interrupted to ask if he could go first. Parker noted the unusual request and asked the reason. Figg stated that his statement might shorten the trial and save all concerned some time. With permission, Figg shocked everybody in the courtroom with his admission that the state was in agreement that the facilities at Clarendon School District Number 22 were inferior to facilities afforded by white students in the district. Adding further that the governor was in agreement with the need to upgrade the facilities and had requested and received approval of the general assembly to provide seventy-five-million-dollar bond through a 0.03 percent sales tax to upgrade facilities for black students in the Clarendon District. Fully exploiting the moment, Figg graciously offered that the state would not oppose the court finding the inequality in the educational opportunities within the black school district for the plaintiffs and issue an injunction prohibiting future violations of the plaintiff's constitutional rights. Figg only asked that the court grant the state time to plan and complete the upgrade of the inadequate facilities under the court's jurisdiction. The surprise had the intended effect with the audience, judges, and Marshall's team.

Marshall quickly recovered and argued "that the statement just made has no bearing on the litigation "because the plaintiffs were asserting that segregation in and of itself is unlawful." He urged the court to allow him to build his case against Clarendon School District. The judges exchanged views, and Waring noted that Figg did not address the issue of segregation being unlawful in his admission even if facilities were equal. He also stated that the plaintiffs had the right to establish their case that segregation was unlawful. Parker concurred and Marshall proceeded making his case.

His strongest evidence was a detailed comparison of white and black schools with photographs that showed the devastating differences between the schools. However, the judges noted that the state already admitted to the inequalities and challenged Marshall to show how segregated schools harmed black students. Marshall placed Dr. Kenneth Clark, a budding psychologist in child development, on the stand to explain the results of his self-esteem experiment on black children using black and white dolls. Clark explained that when black students were asked to answer which doll was smarter, prettier, they always picked the white doll. Clark surprised the court when he told that he had presented the test to the black students in Clarendon District with the same results. Results that indicated psychological harm done to children in inferior schools.

Marshall wrapped his argument around the damage to black children in Clarendon School District because of racially segregated schools and that the children were entitled to equal protection under the law of the Fourteenth Amendment. Figg argued that the same Congress that passed the Fourteenth Amendment also segregated schools in Washington, DC. He asked the court for more time to upgrade facilities for black students in Clarendon District.

Judges Timmerman and Parker agreed to give the state time to upgrade the facilities for black students under the separate but equal doctrine of Plessy. Judge Waring dissented that the state violated the Fourteenth Amendment's equal protection clause and that segregation was "per se" unconstitutional. Because the plaintiffs challenged the constitutionality of the state's school system and the dissent of Judge J. Waites Waring, it guaranteed that the Supreme Court would hear the case. The plaintiffs paid a costly price for the positive outcome, and their courage is a reminder that they paid equal opportunity forward for African Americans.

The Briggs case was sent to the Supreme Court, and in 1952, Clarendon County sent an updated list of improvements to the black school facilities to the Supreme Court. Attorney John W. Davis from South Carolina was the solicitor general and supported separate but equal public schools in the south. Chief Justice Fred Vinson sent the case back to the Eastern District Court of South Carolina for a rehearing. Vinson and three other associate justices were from the south and understood the fierce opposition to ending separate but equal public schools. Thurgood Marshall argued that upgrading the facilities did not matter because the plaintiff's challenge was that separate schools were unconstitutional. The case was then appealed back to the Supreme Court for a rehearing and filed under *Brown v. Board of Education, Topeka*.

The plaintiffs were from Clarendon County and suffered tremendous pressures from the white community for complaining about the dilapidated conditions of their black school. Reverend Joseph DeLaine was a member of the NAACP and a teacher at the black school. He, his wife, daughter, and two nieces—all teachers—were fired by the all-white school board. DeLaine's house caught fire the year prior to the trial, and the volunteer fire department came to the scene but refused to help and watched the house burn to the ground. Harry and Eliza Briggs, lead plaintiffs for the case, also suffered heavy punishment for their support of the petition. Harry, a navy veteran, was a service station attendant and was fired from his job. Eliza, a maid at a motel, was fired from her job. Black farmers in the county were denied loans to plant their crops, and black residents who had outstanding loans were forced to pay them off. The black residents of Clarendon County stood up for themselves despite the intimidation and threats from the white community in the county and across the state of South Carolina. Their gratitude toward Thurgood Marshall and respect for J. Waites Waring would be rewarded when their case was combined with the four other separate but equal cases and successfully argued like theirs as unconstitutional.

Thurgood Marshall's body of legal works, with the assistance of Judge J. Waites Waring, presented the evidence that lead the Supreme Court to dismantle the Plessy doctrine that hampered the education of black students for fifty-eight years. Marshall and Waring embraced the "all men are created equal" concept in the Declaration of Independence and successfully attacked the flawed law that allowed white supremacist to violate the concept and the Fourteenth Amendment to the US Constitution. Marshall has been duly honored with an international airport that bears his name, a college, a law school, a law school library, and a federal judiciary building named after him. The passage of *Brown v. Board of Education, Topeka*, would result from the unexpected death of Chief Justice Vinson and the surprise selection of Earl Warren as his replacement.

Earl Warren, March 19, 1891–July 9, 1964, Los Angeles, California, became the first governor of California to serve three consecutive terms. His appointment as the Chief Justice of the Supreme Court by President Eisenhower on September 30, 1953, surprised many; Warren's rulings surprised President Eisenhower.

As the popular governor of California, Warren considered running for president but changed his mind when Eisenhower's popularity quickly surged throughout the Republican Party. He was also considered a vice presidential candidate, but Eisenhower wanted a younger running mate and chose Richard Nixon, a US senator from California. Warren was not a fan of Nixon but supported Eisenhower in the state of California and at the Republican National Convention. Eisenhower liked Warren and promised him the first open seat on the supreme court. Not knowing when a vacancy would become available and as a good faith gesture, Eisenhower appointed Warren as solicitor general (represents the interest of the United States before the Supreme Court) in 1953. Fate and circumstance intervened to create the first vacancy; Chief Justice Fred Vinson suffered a life-ending heart attack in July 1953. Herbert Brownell, attorney general under Eisenhower, had included Warren's name along with the names of more prominent jurists on the short list to fill the vacancy. Eisenhower had no resistance to Warren's leadership, middle of the road political views, but was concerned over his lack of judicial experience. He wanted a chief justice with integrity and would not use the court to promote a social agenda. Additionally, Eisenhower now had the option to select one of the associate justices to fill the vacancy, but he did not believe any of them had the leadership abilities to handle the tough decisions facing the court's ruling in the pending segregation cases before the court. Eisenhower settled on Warren,[20] believing that Warren was a leader, a man of integrity, popular with republicans, and got along well with him at their short meeting. Warren was sworn in as chief justice on October 30, 1953. Aware that Warren would soon hear the Brown cases, the attorney general prepared a brief on the Justice Department's views of the legality of supporting segregated public schools and concluded that the cases before the Supreme Court could declare the laws unconstitutional. President Eisenhower was informed of the brief and accepted the conclusion without comment. Warren immediately got to work getting to know the eight justices, individually and collectively, and letting them know that he was in charge.

Warren understood the privileges, protocols, and peculiarities of Supreme Court justices. His first act was to schedule a visit in the chambers of Associate Justice Hugo Black, the senior justice. He was congenial and asked Black to introduce him to each of the associate justices in their chambers and to preside over the conferences until he was comfortable with the established procedures and protocols. He quickly established a rapport with each justice, got to assess their style on their turf, and gave them the opportunity to share their concerns. The biggest elephant in the court was *Brown v. Board of Education*, and each justice was eager to informally share their views. Brown maintained his cordiality during his introductory visits and shared his views with each justice in an air of confidence, conviction, and authority. He began presiding over conferences by the end of his visits and scheduled a three-day hearing beginning December 7, 1953, to finally decide whether segregated public schools were unconstitutional.

Thurgood Marshall took the stand and argued that it was time for the court to decide if Plessy would continue to keep Negroes shackled

---

20 James Simon, *Eisenhower vs. Warren: The Battle for Civil Rights and Liberties* (New York: Liveright, 2018), 146.

to slavery or be treated equally under the constitution. Associate Judge Frankfurter, a founding member of the NAACP, pressed Marshall to present the law that allowed the court to overturn Plessy. Marshall cited the Fourteenth Amendment but did not clearly state how the equal protection clause gave the court the authority to declare "separate but equal" unconstitutional. Warren interrupted Marshall once to state, "I would like to have you discuss the question of power because I believe that is the question the Court asked you to discuss." Marshall asked, "The power?" Warren replied, "Yes the power."

Warren had cut to the core of the constitutional challenge. Did the Fourteenth Amendment alone as interpreted by the justices give the court the authority to outlaw public school segregation? Brown knew that neither post-Civil War statues nor court precedents would decide the issue. Neither would a study of the Fourteenth Amendment reveal the framer's intent in application of the law. The attorney general's brief had found that history "inconclusive." Additionally, unbeknownst to Marshall and the other attorney's in the case, Alexander Bickel, law clerk for Justice Douglas and Justice Frankfurter, had also found the history "inconclusive."

John W. Davis, arguing on behalf of the state of South Carolina, took a more pragmatic approach to win over the justices. He recounted the large number of times Plessy had been challenged and sustained as evidence that it was settled law. He also challenged the practical realities that would happen in Clarendon County, South Carolina, if the court integrated public schools. Since the ratio of black to white students in the county was 10 to 1 in the county, he doubted that a class room of twenty-seven black students and three whites would eliminate the psychological burdens of blacks as claimed by Marshall. And he argued that the white children would experience a distorted reality of race relations in America. He concluded his argument by asking the court to preserve "separate but equal" and emphasized the new construction of schools for black children in South Carolina was proof that equal facilities for black children was the best solution for the south and border states in America.

Warren had said little during the hearing, but at their first meeting a week later, he instructed the justices to discuss their views rather than take a vote. He set the stage by sharing his observations of the challenges the court faced in deciding the case. He was of the opinion that the court had to settle the question no matter the desire to avoid the issue. He acknowledged that there were legitimate concerns about reversing Plessy and its progeny. But he said, "The more I've read and heard and thought, the more I've come to conclude that the basis of segregation and 'separate but equal' rests upon a concept of the inherent inferiority of the colored race. I don't see how Plessy and the cases following it can be sustained on any other theory. If we are to sustain segregation, we also must do it on that basis." He quickly clarified his position by stating, "I don't see how in this day and age we can set any group apart from the rest and say that they are not entitled to exactly the same treatment as all others. To do so would be contrary to the Thirteenth, Fourteenth, and Fifteenth Amendments. They were intended to make the slaves equal with all others. Personally, I can't see how today we can justify segregation based solely on race." Warren continued to describe his concerns if the court declared "separate but equal" unconstitutional.

He did not want to inflame public action more than necessary and was not concerned with an order to desegregate schools in Kansas and Delaware where the ethnic population was similar to California's. "But it is not the same in the Deep South," he continued. "It will take all the wisdom of this Court to dispose of the matter with a minimum of emotion and strife. How we do it is important." He ended his concerns by saying that "my instincts and feeling lead me to say that, in these cases, we should abolish the practice of segregation in the public schools—but in a tolerant way." The chief justice's premise that a vote to uphold school segregation could only be justified on the racial theory that black students were inferior compelled the justices to take a stand.

Justice Reed, a Kentucky native, dismissed the argument that the Negro is an inferior race but conceded that lack of opportunity might have hindered their progress. Nonetheless, he urged the court to follow the Plessy precedent. But even while defending Plessy, he recognized that the Constitution was a dynamic document and what was correct that Plessy might not be correct now. Warren still thought that Reed signaled that he could be persuaded.

Justice Tom Clark, a Texan, told Warren that he understood the race problem in the segregated south and was now willing to support a desegregation decision if it was done right and if the remedy could be adjusted to local conditions.

Justice Jackson favored upholding Plessy but signaled that he could agree that the time may have come to end "separate but equal." He was dismissive of the sociological harm to black children and inferred that it would be a decision based on politics rather than law. Warren counted Jackson a maybe and filing a concurrence, disagreeing with the reasoning of the court's opinion.

Justice Frankfurter spoke about there being enough precedent to uphold Plessy, but as a lifetime advocate of racial justice, he was struggling to find a constitutional justification to desegregate the public schools. Warren counted him a supporter.

Justices Black—who was absent, Burton, Douglass, and Minton held to their position in support of a desegregation decree. Warren knew whom he had to work with to reach a unanimous decree. He suggested that the members meet in chambers and over lunch for the next two months to discuss the decision. He was confident in his approach with the justices. He had not thought about how the president would react to a desegregation decision but would soon get his first indication of Eisenhower's interest. He received an invitation to a stag dinner at the White House that disturbed his thoughts about President Eisenhower's interest in the outcome of the court's decision.

On February 8, 1954, Eisenhower hosted a stag dinner at the White House and seated Warren next to himself and within hearing of attorney John W. Davis, who represented South Carolina before Chief Justice Warren and the court just weeks prior. Eisenhower had introduced Davis to Warren as a great man. Later that evening, Eisenhower pulled Warren aside and told him "southerners are not bad people but only concerned that their sweet little girls are not required to sit beside some overgrown Negro." Warren felt that Eisenhower had violated protocol and resented being placed in that awkward position. Nevertheless, he continued to work the issues of desegregation with justices until he was able to gain their unanimous agreement.

May 17, 1954, Warren assembled the associate justices and the press to announce the decision about the future of "separate but equal" in public schools in the southern and border states. He read from a printed sheet and clearly articulated the court's decision to a large and anxious crowd, "We come then to the question presented: Does segregation of children in public schools solely on the basis of race, even though physical facilities and other tangible factors may be equal, deprive the children of the minority group of equal educational opportunities? We unanimously believe that it does… In the field of public education, the doctrine of 'separate but equal' has no place. Separate educational facilities are inherently unequal." The reporters were shocked and, after minutes of absorbing the impact of the decision, scrambled to get the news out to the nation and the world.

African Americans were happy but uncertain of the details of implementation. The court gave no guidance on implementation or when desegregation of public schools was to start. Those details would be announced a year later. White southerners were angry as the ruling confronted them with their dreaded nightmare: having to share their facilities with Negro children who were looked on as inferior in every measure of human evaluation. Warren had struck the central reason for the passage of Plessy in 1896. Some southern white congressional representatives introduced into the Congressional Record the Southern Manifesto—the pledge to fight the Brown decision and overturn the court's ruling. Senator Richard B. Russell (Georgia) and Senator James O. Eastland (Doddsville, Mississippi) gave public statements in the *Washington Post* the day after the announcement that summed up the resistance to the court's ruling. Russell, head of the Senate's Southern Democratic caucus angrily charged the court is becoming the "pliant tool" of the executive Department, and said, "Ways must be found to check the tendency of the Court to disregard the Constitution and the precedents of able and unbiased judges…" Eastland was even more defiant and declared the south "will not abide by nor obey this legislative decision by a political court," adding, "we will take whatever steps are necessary to retain segregation in education." The second paragraph in the editorial in that same paper sought to explain and critique Chief Justice Warren's reasoning behind the decision. "The Chief Justice's twin opinions in the segregation cases informed by a compelling logic. They eradicate, and unequivocally, the "separate but equal" doctrine contrived by the Supreme Court nearly sixty years ago in *Plessy v. Ferguson*. The Dred Scott decision excepted, no shabbier judicial proposition has ever been enunciated than Mr. Justice Warren's that "the enforced separation of the two races stamps the colored race with a badge of inferiority...solely because the colored race chooses to put that construction upon it."

Monday's decision is a resounding vindication of the wisdom expressed by Mr. Justice Harlan in his eloquent dissent in the Plessy case: "In view of the Constitution, in the eye of the law, there is in this country no superior, dominant, ruling class of citizens. There is no caste here. Our Constitution is color-blind, and neither knows nor tolerates classes among citizens." Justice Harlan was eloquent and outnumbered in 1896 and dissented—Justice Warren named racism by the white majority as the justification of "separate but equal" and based his justification on the principle of the Declaration of Independence to dismantle Plessy with a unanimous decision. For most Americans, the Declaration of Independence ranks the US Constitution in purpose and seniority. I guess the justices added the violation of the equal protection clause under the Fourteenth Amendment to satisfy the legal precedent in the US Constitution.

Earl Warren changed America for the better. Many branded him an activist using the court to create social change in civil liberties, civil rights, and equal rights. I brand him an American role model because of his modest beginning, as a first-generation son of an immigrant, willing to work through adverse circumstances to improve himself, his community, and ultimately his country. Warren was a situational leader devoted to fixing or finding solutions to problems that affected people. As attorney for Alameda County, California, attorney general of California, three-term California governor and Chief Justice of the Supreme Court, Warren found people friendly solutions. In the California of his era—where the situation required cleaning up bribery, get rich quick schemes, and equal protection under the law—he delivered, cleaning toxic waste from Los Angeles beaches, establishing hospital care within a mile of radius of each resident, and a host of other firsts for California residents. The Supreme Court required a chief justice with the right combination of intellect, courage, and leadership skills to make laws that follow America's best founding principle in the Declaration of Independence—he provided that too. I and millions of Americans are beneficiaries of the opportunities presented by the desegregation of public schools. My introduction shares my opportunities and the history books, corporate offices, school systems, court rooms, farms and factories, and religious institutions have also benefited from Earl Warren's contributions to America's journey. Although Warren's contributions in the civil rights arena ruffled feelings, and inflamed emotions, President Eisenhower did not use the full office to support the decision. He only did his duty when Governor Orval Faubus refused to obey a district court order to allow nine black children to attend Central High School in Little Rock, Arkansas.

Dwight David Eisenhower, October 14, 1890, Denison, Texas—March 28, 1969, thirty-fourth President of the United States.

The first opportunity President Eisenhower had to speak about the Supreme Court's *Brown v. Topeka* ruling was at a press conference a week after Supreme Court Chief Justice Warren announced the decision on May 17, 1954. Eisenhower's only comment was that it was the law of the land, and he hoped it would be obeyed. After Warren announced the details of implementation in Brown II— with all deliberate speed—Eisenhower again stated that he hoped that the law would be obeyed. He also added that he understood the emotional changes southern white people were going through and understood that it would take time for them to adjust. Eisenhower's peculiar and ambivalent attitude about racial integration had the effect of empathizing with the southern senators, governors, and white citizen councils' efforts to undermine Brown and the authority of the Supreme Court. Eisenhower's conflicted attitude about race and confrontation with Governor Faubus and the Little Rock School integration in 1957 reveals the power of white southern politicians to use white supremacy for their own political survival. Eisenhower courted the southern vote during his campaign and valued his friendships with Governor James Byrnes, South Carolina, and others.

Eisenhower campaigned heavily in the south and emphasized his support of state's rights. He made it clear that his policy on civil rights was to enforce the laws in organizations that the federal government controlled and respected states' rights. He received the support of Governor James Byrnes who campaigned and voted for him in the state. Byrnes, a former 7 term US Congressman SC, US senator, Associate Supreme Court Justice, Director of War Mobilization and Secretary of State, ran for Governor to preserve public school segregation in his state. Shortly after Eisenhower took office Byrnes asked for and had lunch at the White House with Eisenhower. The topic was to discuss the supreme court cases on public schools. Byrnes told the president that South Carolina would close public schools rather than let their children mix with black students in schools. Eisenhower responded to Byrnes' concerns in a letter and wrote the contents of his response to Byrnes in his diary. He essentially informed him of his thoughts and intentions on matters of race and equality[21]: "I told him that while I was not going to give in advance my attitude toward a Supreme Court opinion I had not even seen and so could not know in what terms it would be couched." He also emphasized that his "convictions would not be formed by political expediency." He believed that the best result would be achieved by cooperation between the federal government and the states, and not by a federal law that imposed a solution on the states. He doubted that coercion by the federal government would be effective and agreed with Byrnes that improvement in race relations required local support. "Consequently, I believe that Federal law imposed upon our states in such a way as to bring about a conflict of the police powers of the states and of the nation would set back the cause of progress in race relations for a long, long, time," he told Byrnes. He also urged Byrnes

---

[21]   James Simon, *Eisenhower vs. Warren: The Battle for Civil Rights and Liberties* (New York: Liveright, 2018), 128–129.

to communicate his stance on civil rights with his fellow southern governors. The Brown decision would strain relationships between Eisenhower and Byrnes and the other southern governors.

Eisenhower's stance was much more assertive on his role to uphold civil rights when campaigning in northern states. He promised that he would use the power of his office to break down racial barriers controlled by the federal government, including the District of Columbia. In his first months as president, he acted decisively in directing his attorney general, Herbert Brownell, to desegregate restaurants in DC and the secretaries of the military services in the Defense Department to integrate on post military schools wherever such schools were operated under military funding and control. He was confident of his authority as commander-in-chief to compel compliance with equal rights laws that did not intrude on the state's right to govern institutions under their control. He appeared less sure of his authority to compel American citizens, and especially southern whites, to obey the laws of the court. By contrast, Chief Justice Warren was confident that the court had the authority to interpret and decide the laws under the constitution of the United States for the American people. He felt strongly that the executive and legislative branches of government were sworn to uphold the laws of the court. Brown and Brown II critically tested the elected members of both the legislative and executive branch to put aside their racial bias and enforce the court's decision.

The Brown ruling that separate schools for white and black students were unconstitutional was met with massive resistance by southern governors and congressional representatives. The Brown II ruling that schools would be integrated with all deliberate speed under district court approval was met with outright defiance in Georgia, Louisiana, Mississippi, and South Carolina. One hundred and one members of Congress signed a Southern Manifesto declaring that Brown was a clear abuse of judicial power. Impeach Earl Warren and the Supreme Court signs were prominent in southern states. When Eisenhower was asked about the Southern Manifesto, he once again hoped that the states would obey the law but expressed his understanding of how white southerners could be angry and confused; for years the Supreme Court had upheld that segregation was legal and moral, and Brown says it is not. He sympathized that they just need time. The major newspapers in the south published editorials agreeing that the court's decision to integrate public schools with all deliberate speed under purview of the district courts was reasonable and encouraged communities to proceed in good faith. Little Rock, Arkansas, was not among the states railing against the court's decision but became the focal point and test case for Eisenhower and the executive branch of government.

When Brown II was announced in 1955, Faubus voiced no concerns or issues with the decision. The Little Rock School board submitted a plan to the district court for nine black students to integrate to Central High School in the fall of 1957. The nine black students were from middle class families, had above average grades, and the district court approved the integration plan. Faubus was up for reelection in 1958 and became concerned about his support of school integration just days before Central High was scheduled to open.

Faubus was from a poor Arkansas family, dropped out of school after the eighth grade, did menial jobs until going into the army in World War II, completed high school through GED, became an officer, and achieved the rank of major. Being the governor was the best job he ever held, and he feared that he could not land a comparable salaried job if he was defeated. Having served in army intelligence during the war, he had a good political network and learned that his opponents were going to run against racial integration and become governor of Arkansas. To change his stance on the integration plan, Faubus started to manufacture rumors that hostile crowds were going to interfere with the integration of Central High School. He was also visited by Governors Eastland of Mississippi and Griffin of Georgia, and the leaders of the white Citizens' Council. Both governors were fierce opponents of Brown I and II and were closing public schools in their states to keep from complying with the court's ruling. Faubus decided to use his manufactured crisis to keep the nine black students from entering Central High School.

On September 3, 1957, school opening day at Central High, Faubus called up the Arkansas National Guard to ostensibly guard against unruly armed protesters, but his unpublicized direct order was to deny entry to the black students. The school board learned of Faubus's action the morning of the school opening and called the parents of the nine black students to keep the student's home. The television cameras and a large crowd occupied the headlines across the nation. The mayor of Little Rock denounced Faubus's manufactured fears, and the school board requested instructions from the district court judge. The judge would not delay the plan. The ball was now in Eisenhower's court.

Eisenhower held a press conference and was asked about the school situation in Little Rock. He weakly supported Brown but did not believe federal force was appropriate and stated that the Justice Department was sending the FBI to assess the threat of armed protesters. He reiterated the futility of anyone who believed that laws could change the hearts and minds of people. He further elaborated that "there are very strong emotions on the other side, people that see a picture of mongrelization of the race, they call it." His attorney general, Brownell, urged Eisenhower to enforce Brown II as he saw Little Rock as a test case for the southern states. All sides were locked into their positions; Faubus was committed to keeping the peace under his state constitution, the district court and schoolboard was standing behind it's school integration plan, and Eisenhower did not want to use federal force.

September 4, 1957, brought out the best and worse in the struggle to integrate Central High School. Two hundred plus National Guard troops surround the high school. The school board with the assistance of Daisy Bates, NAACP, the Little Rock School Board, and mayor of Little Rock arrange for the Little Rock Nine to attend their first day of school at Central High. Bates used her home as the meeting place for the students and arranged for the nine to be escorted to the school by eight ministers (four black and four white) with a city police car to move slowly with them. As the student and escorts neared the school, a crowd of four hundred jeering whites begin hurling racial slurs. "Go home niggers!" they yelled. "Two, four, six, eight, we ain't gonna integrate," they chanted. When the students arrived at the entrance, a National Guard Captain armed with a rifle and bayonet announced that by order of Governor Faubus, the students would not be allowed to enter the school. Once the crowd realized the National Guard was there to deny students entry, they became more embolden in their jeers and chants. One of the students, fifteen-year-old Elizabeth Eckford, did not get the message to meet at Bates's house and began walking toward the school. She saw the crowd and the troops and assumed the troops were there for her protection. As she approached, the crowd hurled epithets at her and two National Guard Soldiers blocked her path with crossed bayonets. The crowd yelled, "Lynch her!" The fifteen-year-old five feet tall Elizabeth became terrified and retreated to a bench at a bus stop about one hundred yards away. She was visibly shaken when she was seated on the bench at the bus stop. An elderly white woman set beside her and put her arms around her until the bus carried them away from the harrowing scene. Faubus was now openly defying the order to integrate Central High School.

Faubus became embolden over the next three weeks. He held a press conference announcing that no black students would integrate any high schools in the city as long as he was governor of the state; he resisted compliance with the district court orders; telegraphed Eisenhower to remove FBI agents from the state so they would not interfere with his state constitutional duty of keeping the peace, and that he would not cooperate with the FBI. Eisenhower was on vacation in Rhode Island and replied by telegram that he would uphold the federal Constitution "by every means at my command." The president reaffirmed that the Justice Department was there to help and not to interfere with his state constitutional duties. He also let the governor know that the federal government shared in funding the National Guard's uniforms and equipment. Faubus telegraphed back that he would uphold the constitution of Arkansas and the nation. A veld threat of his continued resistance. Attorney General Brownell, acting as a friend of the court, filed a temporary injunction to halt Faubus's action in deploying National Guard troops at Central High School to prevent integration. District Judge Davies set September 20 as the date for Faubus to appear in his courtroom to defend his actions. Meanwhile a search for a solution broadens.

Congressman Hays of Arkansas believes that Faubus is looking for a way to end the crisis and contacts Eisenhower's chief of staff to propose a meeting with Eisenhower. The president did not want to side with Faubus nor appear to be a party to the federal suit. He wanted to assure Faubus that the federal government would not interfere with the legitimate responsibilities of the governor to preserve order. The president instructed his chief of staff and Brownell to help Faubus prepare a telegram requesting the meeting and stating that he (Faubus) would "obey all proper orders of our courts." Faubus verbally agreed with the wording but modified the telegram sent to Eisenhower with his pledge to obey District Judge Davies's order "consistent with my responsibilities under the Constitution of the United States and that of Arkansas." By this time the FBI's report of Faubus claims of armed protesters posing a threat to the peace of Little Rock was without evidence. Brownell informed Eisenhower of the report's findings and reemphasized that Faubus was only interested in winning a third term as governor and had no intention of obeying the order. Eisenhower accepted the conclusion but agreed to meet with Faubus as a last-ditch effort to avoid a military confrontation over racial integration of public schools in Little Rock.

Eisenhower and Faubus met privately Saturday morning, September 14, 1957, for about twenty minutes in a small office at a naval base in Newport, Rhode Island. They moved to a larger office where Eisenhower's chief of staff, Brownell, Congressman Hays, and reporters were present. Eisenhower summarized the meeting as cordial and constructive with the governor agreeing to comply with the court's order. He even complimented the governor for cooperating to resolve the difficult process. Eisenhower even asked Brownell if the governor's court appearance could be delayed a couple of weeks. Brownell's reply was a decisive "No, the governor must comply with the court order." Faubus listened in stunned silence to Brownell's answer. Faubus agreed that the meeting was constructive but emphasized the difficulties of complying with the order and harmonizing his actions with the state. Pictures were taken of the president and the governor both smiling. Eisenhower returned to the gold course, and Faubus returned to Little Rock.

Faubus held an interview with ABC television reporter Mike Wallace when he returned to Little Rock. He continued to warn of the danger of violence. When Wallace asked why he didn't use the National Guard to escort the nine students to class and end the problem, Faubus intimated that the nine were the problem. Eisenhower, seeing and hearing Faubus on national television, realized that he had been "double-crossed" but was still reluctant to send troops. Brownell advised Eisenhower to wait until after Faubus's meeting with District Court Judge Davies on September 20. On the morning of the hearing, Faubus's attorneys asked Judge Davies to rescue himself because of his bias against their client. The judge dismissed their request and issued an injunction against Faubus to stop blocking the integration of Central High School. The attorneys walked out of the court. Faubus told the press that he was going to appeal Judge Davies's injunction. He also ordered the National Guard to withdraw from the school on Monday morning when the school opened and informed the press that he was attending a southern governor's conference on Sea Island, Georgia, over the weekend.

Brownell advised Eisenhower of the news and advised that the president must act. Eisenhower weighed the range of reactions from other southern governors, did not want to set off a chain reaction to his use of troops, and decided to put a positive spin on Faubus's decision to withdraw the National Guard on that Monday, September 23. His statement complemented the governor's decision to remove the troops and summarized that the citizens of Little Rock will welcome the opportunity for their state to comply with the proper orders of the United States Courts.

Monday morning, September 23, 1957, all hell broke loose. A mob of about one thousand white protesters, included the Ku Klux Klan, the White Citizens' Council, and the state athletic commissioner and close friend of Faubus surrounded the school. They beat and kicked two black reporters covering the story and chanted their displeasure of black students attending Central High School. Amid the mob's attention on the black reporters, the nine black students were snuck into a side door of the school. The crowd became even more outraged when they learned of the black students being in the school. Little Rock's Mayor Mann, fearing for the safety of the students, ordered the city police to escort the black students out of the school. The Little Rock School integration story dominated the news, and the White House received cables from around the world stating that the Little Rock story was a public affairs disaster. Even the Russians seized the opportunity to label America hypocrisy in promoting democracy and human rights around the world while tolerating racism and bigotry at home. Eisenhower knew he had to act but was still paralyzed over how the south would react to his use of troops.

On the afternoon of the 23rd, Eisenhower issued a blunt warning that anarchy would not be permitted and that he would use force if necessary to enforce the orders of the courts. He cited his authority under the constitution to use force and ended with his customary appeal to the law-abiding citizens to obey the law.

The next morning, in an extraordinary appeal for help, Little Rock mayor, Woodrow Wilson Mann, telegrammed the president of the United States for help. His urgent message bypassed all state and federal layers of government to the elected official granted the power to act. Straight and to the point, it read:

> The immediate need for federal troops is urgent.
> The mob is much larger in numbers at 8 a.m. than
> at any time yesterday. People are converging on
> the scene from all directions. Mob is armed and
> engaging in fisticuffs and other acts of violence.
> Situation is out of control and the police cannot
> disperse the mob.

Faced with insurrection, the president knew he had to act to restore law and order. The fact that he was still on vacation in Rhode Island while the crisis exploded concerned him from a public image point of view. He was in constant contact with Attorney General Brownell who had coordinated with General Maxwell Taylor, chief of staff of the army, to recommend the best troops to restore law and order. Taylor recommended the National Guard. Eisenhower didn't want to "pit brother against brother" reminiscent of the Civil War, so he initially ruled out federalizing the Little Rock National Guard troops in favor of guard troops from another part of Arkansas. Brownell had also prepared a statement for Eisenhower that began with "The law has been defied," but the president preferred an opening statement that empathized with the people of the law abiding south. Later the afternoon of September 24, 1957, Eisenhower called Brownell to say that he had changed his mind and wanted to send active army troops along with federalizing the Arkansas National Guard. The president called General Taylor at 12:15 p.m., and within hours, five hundred troops from the 101st Airborne "Screaming Eagles" landed at Little Rock, Arkansas, and by nightfall five hundred more were on the ground. Taylor, a native Missourian and West Point graduate, commanded and parachuted with the division into Normandy during WWII. Eisenhower's decision to deploy troops to protect the equal rights of African Americans was the first time since the Civil War.

Eisenhower flew back to the White House the evening of September 24 to address the nation. He told his radio and television audience that he used federal troops to stop "anarchy" and restore order. He also emphasized that the troops were in Little Rock to enforce a court order, not integration. And he appealed to the citizens of Little Rock to return to their normal habits of obeying the laws to return to peace and restore the image of America. Outrage from southern governors and senators was swift and unanimous in their charge that the president was destroying the social order of the south. Faubus went on national television to announce that Arkansas was an occupied territory.

On the morning of September 25, 1957, thirty soldiers of the 101st Airborne Division—without its black soldiers (they rejoined the division after Little Rock)—escorted the nine black students into Central High School. Twenty-four soldiers of the 101st patrolled the halls as the black students attended classes with their white classmates. The 101st dispersed the crowd outside the school and remained at Central High School until Thanksgiving 1957. The Arkansas National Guard remained at the school until the end of the school year in 1958.[22] Faubus closed the public high schools in

---

22   "Little Rock Nine," Wikipedia, last updated April 6, 2019, https://en.wiki-pedia.org/wiki/Little_Rock_Nine#%22The_Lost_Year%22.

Little Rock 1958-1959 to prevent racial integration. His appeal to racism was embraced by the Arkansas Legislature, Little Rock School board, and the majority of citizens in Little Rock who supported Faubus's referendum to keep the schools closed. The school board replaced the three proponents of racial segregation on the board and challenged Faubus to reopen the schools and comply with the district court's integration order. The public high schools reopened in 1959–1960. The black community was blamed for the school difficulties in Little Rock, and therefore the black students faced hostility when the schools reopened. The power of racism to destroy a community is an unflattering legacy of Little Rock.

The ambivalence of President Eisenhower over the issue of equality for all citizens as a right under the constitution of the United States and his reluctance to enforce the Supreme Court's orders to protect the rights of the disenfranchised is a legacy of white supremacy in America. Throughout the ordeal of Faubus's resistance to the district court's order to comply with Brown II, Eisenhower made no effort to defend the Brown decision on constitutional or moral grounds.[23] "Chief Justice Warren was dismayed by Eisenhower's reticence. Even after the president sent troops to Little Rock," Warren noted, "there was no direct appeal from the White House to obey the mandate of the Supreme Court." Eisenhower's concerns over white southerners' feelings appeared to weigh more heavily than African Americans' rights under the constitution. In that regard, his views of constitutional equality favored separate but equal for African Americans. Thankfully, he appointed Earl Warren to be chief justice of the Supreme Court and Herbert Brownell Jr., attorney general of the Justice Department. Warren recognized that the greatness of America was its unique promise to all citizens in the Declaration of Independence. He was able to persuade his fellow justices to denounce supporting laws on the basis of racism and to approve laws on the basis of the moral truth derived from the Declaration of Independence. Eisenhower, the chief of the executive branch, was forced to choose between a law of racism or a law of morality.

---

23   James Simon, *Eisenhower vs. Warren: The Battle for Civil Rights and Liberties* (New York: Liveright, 2018), 308–309.

Brownell recognized the president's reticence to enforce Brown and Brown II and showed courage and determination to push the president to enforce the law. District Judge Davies and Little Rock mayor Woodrow Wilson Mann also deserve credit for pulling Eisenhower past his ambivalence to enforce the law. Eisenhower did his duty to enforce Brown, perhaps the most significant equal rights law since the Thirteenth, Fourteenth, and Fifteenth Amendments to the Constitution in shaping American toward the country envisioned under the Declaration of Independence. Southern resistance to racial and social equality would dominate American domestic policy under Presidents Kennedy and Johnson.

John Fitzgerald Kennedy (May 29, 1917–November 22, 1963), Thirty-Fifth President, United States of America, and Lyndon Baines Johnson (August 27, 1908—January 22, 1973) Thirthy-Sixth President, United States of America

Eisenhower's successor would have to deal with a southern democratic party that was openly rebelling against civil rights laws that eroded the social order between white and black southerners. Because of Brown I and II, public schools were closed in many of the deep southern states. Eisenhower's 1960 voting rights bill added to the friction between the federal government and state's rights. Vice President Richard Nixon was the uncontested candidate for the Republican Party's nomination. Senators John Kennedy, Lyndon Johnson and Adlai Stevenson II, and Hubert Humphries wanted the Democratic nomination. Kennedy's superior organization and financial backing of his father, Joe Kennedy, won him the nomination. He and Richard Nixon fought a closely contested race for the right to succeed Eisenhower.

Kennedy narrowly defeated Nixon in the popular vote and won 309 to Nixon's 219 electoral votes to become president. Fourteen electors from Mississippi and Alabama refused to vote for Kennedy because of his support of the civil rights movement. Realizing his unpopularity in the south, Kennedy choose Senator Lyndon Johnson, Texas, as his vice president over the objection of his brother and family members. His inaugural address set the stage for the future while working to improve equal rights in America.

Kennedy thrilled Americans and people around the world with his ability to turn a phrase into a lasting memory. "Ask not what your country can do for you. Ask what you can do for your country." I was a first lieutenant at Fort Leonard Wood, Missouri, and can still remember the pride I felt from hearing the phrase. My step had a bigger bounce when Kennedy was in office. He included his support of civil rights in the state of the union message and promised to end racial discrimination. His appointment of Thurgood Marshall to the Court of Appeals in the Second Circuit was a welcome sign of his commitment to civil rights. Then the defeat of his Appalachian program by southern democrats made him realize the nexus between passing his proposed legislation in Congress and his support of black civil rights protests. Black protests of discrimination in lunch counters, bus transportation, water fountains, and school admissions tested his use of force to enforce the law and maintain the peace.

James Meredith, a United States Air Force veteran, was inspired by President Kennedy's inaugural address and decided to exercise his constitutional right to enroll at the University of Mississippi. In September 1962, Meredith enrolled at the university and was denied admission by Governor Ross Barnett, who had appointed himself register of the university for that purpose. Barnett made television address to adamantly state that racial integration would never be allowed in Mississippi as long as he was governor. Attorney General Robert F. Kennedy set up conversations with Barnett to diffuse the situation and persuade the governor to cooperate. Barnett needed a face-saving gesture, and the attorney general sent three hundred federal marshals to escort Meredith into the university. Rioting and violence erupted with armed protesters firing at escorts to prevent Meredith from enrolling. President Kennedy reluctantly sent in three thousand federal troops from the Second Division, commanded by Brigadier General Charles Billingslea, and US Army Military Police from the 503rd and 716th MP Battalions, plus elements from the US Border Patrol and the federalized Mississippi National Guard.

Attorney General Robert Kennedy quietly arranged for the black troops of the participating units to remain at their duty stations. Former Major General Edwin A. Walker (John Birch Society believer—resigned his commission after thirty years of service) rallied the mob and urged them to protect the sovereignty of Mississippi. Billingslea's car was fired on and set on fire when he arrived on campus. He, his deputy commanding general, John Corley, his military aide, Captain Harold, Lyon and his driver managed to get out of the burning car and were fired on as they crawled for cover at the University Lyceum Building. The army did not return fire. Two men were murdered during the first night of the riots: a French journalist found behind the Lyceum with a gunshot wound in the back, and a jukebox repairman who visited the campus out of curiosity was found with a bullet wound in his forehead. Law enforcement officials described these as execution-style killings.

Meredith was finally admitted to the university on October 1, 1962, and became the first African American to graduate from the university on August 18, 1963. During his entire time on campus, Meredith was guarded twenty-four hours every day. The Kennedy administration met that challenge of racism but would be tested throughout the south. The month of June 1963 would be a trying time for civil rights activists and the Kennedy administration.

June 11, 1963, Alabama governor George Wallace brazenly defied a federal district judge's court order to comply with Brown II.

Following *Brown v. Board* ruling in 1954, hundreds of applicants applied for admission to the University of Alabama but were denied on various technicalities or intimidated to quit trying. In early June 1963, Vivian Malone and James Hood applied for enrollment at the University of Alabama and were denied on the basis of their race. The federal district court judge ordered the university to let them enter the university. Attorney General Robert Kennedy sent Deputy Attorney General Nicholas Katzenbach and federal marshals to escort the black students into the university. Alabama governor George Wallace, who had campaigned on the slogan "Segregation Now, Segregation Tomorrow, and Segregation Forever" stood in front of the entrance of Foster Hall to deny the students entry. Katzenbach asked the governor to remove himself and comply with a presidential proclamation ordering the state to comply with the court's order. Wallace refused, stating the order had no legal force, and began speaking about state's rights. Katzenbach called President Kennedy, who issued an Executive Order 11110 federalizing the Alabama National Guard and directing Major General Henry Graham, the commanding general, to comply with the court order. General Graham approached Wallace, saluted, and told him, "Sir, it is my sad duty to ask you to step aside under the orders of the president of the United States." Wallace continued to speak but eventually moved aside. Katzenbach escorted Malone and Hood inside Foster Hall, where they were registered without incident. The guard remained under federal control and was used to assist in the integration of public schools across the state of Alabama. The guard remained under federal control because Wallace refused to be a party to integrating the schools in Alabama. Kennedy used the moment to advance his civil rights initiatives.

On the night of June 11, Kennedy gave a televised report to the American people on his civil rights initiatives and to highlight Wallace's attempts to prevent two black students from attending the University of Alabama. He cited the American belief that all are created equal and have a right to attend public schools and universities. The president also discussed how discrimination affected public safety, international relations, and the nation's image of preaching freedom internationally and denying it domestically. He concluded by asking Congress to pass legislation to provide greater support for access to public schools and other facilities and greater protection for voter rights. His initiative would become the centerpiece of the Civil Rights Act of 1964. His report was well received by civil rights activists but hardened the resolve of white supremacist.

Medgar Evers, a WWII veteran and NAACP state field secretary in Mississippi, was shot and killed in front of his home in Jackson, Mississippi, on June 12. The assassin was a member of the white Citizens' Council and was acquitted by a white jury.

The *New York Times* editorial on June 16 argued that the Kennedy administration moved too slow and with little evidence of moral commitment on civil rights. "He now demonstrates a genuine sense of urgency about eradicating racial discrimination from our national life." Kennedy celebrated the March on Washington in August 1963 and mourned the deaths of three black girls from the bombing of the church in Birmingham, Alabama, in September 1963. His presidency was ended by Lee Harvey Oswald, in Dallas, Texas, November 22, 1963.

Lyndon Baines Johnson was sworn in as the thirty-sixth president of the United States on Air Force One, November 22, 1963, at Love Field, Dallas, Texas, after the assassination of President Kennedy. He was administered the oath of office by Sarah T. Hughes, judge of the district court for the Northern District of Texas. She is the only woman to swear in a president of the United States. And Johnson is the only president sworn into the presidency on Air Force One.

Johnson was eager to prove that he could move the Congress to pass legislation. He had served as the senate minority leader and senate majority leader respectively and was known to be ruthless, cunning, and charming with representatives to get their vote. As a member of the house and senate, Johnson had aligned himself with the southern caucus and opposed legislation favorable to African Americans. As vice president, Johnson attempted to use his political skills to help President Kennedy but was politely kept out of the process. As president, Johnson eagerly used his political skills and connections to move Kennedy's civil rights bill through the legislative process. He signed the bill into law, July 2, 1964. On the matters of civil rights, Johnson moved away from his southern democrat allies to become one of the most effective champions on civil rights for African Americans.

After consolidating his power and defeating Barry Goldwater in the 1964 presidential election, Johnson became a champion of civil rights in America. The events leading up to and the passage of the Voting Rights Act of 1965 defined his domestic goals as president and endeared him to African Americans throughout most of his term as president.

The voting registration drive by Martin Luther King Jr. and civil rights organizations in Selma, Alabama, in January 1965 caught Johnson by surprise. He was expecting a longer period of celebration after the passage of the Civil Rights Act of 1964 and a time to allow white southerners to adjust to the historic freedoms the act offered to African Americans. But King informed Johnson of his intention to use the protests as a means to demand the African American's constitutional right to vote. Johnson, according to Joseph A. Califono, Head of Domestic Affairs for Johnson 1965–1969, considered King essential in getting his Voting Rights Bill passed. As the protest marches in Selma and the surrounding counties progressed on March 7, March 9, and March 21–25, tensions mounted and Johnson masterfully intervened to protect the marchers and urge passage of the Voting Rights bill. The impetus for the Selma to Montgomery march was Jimmie Lee Jackson, a US veteran and deacon in his church. Jackson had been killed by a police officer while peacefully protesting in Marion, Alabama, on February 26, 1965, as part of the local march organizers, Dallas County Voters League (DCVL).

To gain more attention to their cause, the DCVL decided to use a longer protest route from Selma to Montgomery—and invite Martin Luther King Jr to lead the effort. The first March on the 7th, the marchers were met by local police, county posse men swinging billy clubs, dogs, tear gas. The marchers turned back before reaching the Edmund Pettis Bridge to Montgomery. The second march on the 9th, the marchers included white civil rights advocates from across the United States. The marches made it to the end of the Pettus Bridge before encountering the state troopers and local police force. The troopers stepped aside, but Martin Luther King, following the injunction by the federal district judge, turned around and led the marchers back to the local church.

That night, a local mob beat to death James Reeb, a Boston Unitarian minister. The media and civil rights across the US demanded protection for the marchers and called for a voting rights act to grant African Americans their constitutional right to vote. Alabama governor George Wallace refused to provide protection and requested a meeting with President Johnson.[24] Wallace was not persuaded by the president's powerful argument of the marcher's constitutional rights to peaceful assembly, voting rights, and his responsibility to keep the peace. After the large outcry over the murder of Reeb, Johnson federalized the Alabama National Guard and augmented them with US Marshals to protect the marchers along the fifty-four-mile route to Montgomery. Johnson also used the event to address a joint session of Congress that was nationally televised.

March 15, 1965, President Johnson delivered a demanding and persuasive message to a joint session of congress and the American people on the need to provide constitutional rights to African Americans. He also used the event to state the kind of president he wanted to be for all Americans. Excerpts highlight his message to Americans and masterful manipulation of the congress:

> I speak tonight for the dignity of man and the destiny of democracy.[25]
>
> There is no cause for pride in what happened in Selma. There is no cause for self-satisfaction in the long denial of equal rights of millions of Americans, but there is cause for hope and for faith in our democracy in what is happening here tonight.
>
> Experience has clearly shown that the existing process of law cannot overcome systematic and ingenious discrimination. No law that we now have on the books—and I helped to put three of them there—can ensure the right to vote when local officials are determined to deny it.
>
> The constitution says that no person shall be kept from voting because of his race or his color. We have all sworn an oath before God to

---

[24]   Doris Kearns Goodwin, *Lyndon Johnson and the American Dream* (New York: Open Road Media, 2015).

[25]   The Public Papers of the President of the United States, "Lyndon B Johnson: 1965," (Washington, DC: Government Printing Office, 1966), vol. 1, entry 107, pp. 281–287.

support and defend that Constitution. We must now act in obedience to that oath.

Wednesday, I will send to congress a law designed to eliminate illegal barriers to the right to vote.

The broad principles if that bill will be in the hands of the Democratic and Republican leaders tomorrow. After they have reviewed it, it will come here formally as a bill. I am grateful for this opportunity to come here tonight at the invitation of the leadership to reason with my friends, to give them my views, and to visit with my former colleagues.

This bill will strike down restrictions to voting in all elections—federal, state, and local—which have been used to deny Negroes the right to vote. This bill will establish a simple, uniform standard which cannot be used, however ingenious the effort, to flout our constitution. It will provide for citizens to be registered by officials of the United States Government if the state officials refuse to register them. It will eliminate tedious, unnecessary law suits which delay the right to vote. Finally, this legislation will ensure that properly registered individuals are not prohibited from voting.

I want to be the President who: educated young children to the wonders of their world; helped feed the hungry and to prepare them to be tax payers instead of taxeaters; helped the poor to find their own way and who protected the right of every citizen to vote in every election; helped to end hatred among his fellow men and who promoted love among people of all races and all regions and all parties, and helped to end war among brothers of this earth.

Johnson ended his speech by explaining that the Latin words above the great seal of the United States means "God has favored our undertaking." He opined that God may not favor everything we do but believed that God truly favored the undertaking that they began that night. Reaction to the speech was generally favorable.

Many civil rights activists were overwhelmed with emotion that a president of the United states would act on their behalf to secure their long hard fight for voting rights. Others like J. L. Chestnut, a Selma activist, feared that Johnson had "outfoxed" and "co-opted" King and the SCLC.

The *New York Times* editorial, capturing the historical perspective of the speech, wrote:, "No other American president had so completely identified himself with the cause of the Negro. No other President had made the issue of equality for Negroes so frankly a moral cause to himself and all Americans." Johnson had accomplished his role and set the stage for King to do his part.

Six days later, Martin Luther King Jr. and thousands of marchers departed Selma on March 21 and, with encampments along the way, arrived in Montgomery on March 25—without incident along the fifty-four-mile route. President Johnson signed the Voting Rights Bill into law on August 6, 1965. The act increased black voters in all southern states. And in Alabama in 1960, only 53,000 blacks were registered, and by 1990, more than 530,000 blacks were registered voters. Historians credit Johnson with courage and foresight in advancing the cause of democracy in America. The Vietnam War and race riots from 1965 to 1968 damaged his standing among historians. I believe President Johnson championed the cause of civil rights on behalf of African Americans as a means to gain favor and fame as the thirty-sixth president of the United States. His disappointment over the riots that tarnished his civil rights accomplishments provide insight of his racial beliefs about African Americans and their collective behavior.

Doris Kearns, in her book *Lyndon Johnson and the American Dream*, provides context and Johnson's comments about his frustrations with Negroes and minorities. Speaking of Watts and the riots that followed, Kearns said, "Watts was the precursor of more than one hundred riots that stretched out for three long summers, leaving 225 people dead, 4,000 wounded, and $112 billion in property damage. Initially, Johnson perceived only the harm the rioters had done to him, seeing in the flames of the stores and the houses his own betrayal." Johnson was quoted as saying, "It simply wasn't fair for a few irresponsible agitators to spoil it for me and for all the rest of the Negroes, who are basically peace-loving and nice. A few hoodlums sparked by outside agitators who moved around from city to city making trouble. Spoiling all the progress I've made in these last few years."

Kearns continued that sometimes Johnson seemed to understand the frustrations of Negroes and never admitting his part in creating that frustration. Johnson said,

> God knows how little we've really moved on this issue, despite all the fanfare. As I see it, I've moved the Negro from D+ to C- He's still nowhere. He knows it. And that's why he's out in the street. Hell, I'd be there too. It was bad enough in the south—especially from the standpoint of education—but at least there the Negro knew he was really loved and cared for, which he never was in the North, where children live with rats and have no place to sleep and come from broken homes and get rejected from the Army. And then they look on TV and see all the promises of a rich country and they know that some movement is beginning to take place in their lives, so they begin to hope for a lot more. Hell, when a person's released from jail or his parents, it is only natural that he takes advantage and turns to excess. Remember the Negroes in Reconstruction who got elected to Congress and then ran into the chamber with bare feet and white women. They were simply not prepared for their responsibility. And we weren't just or kind enough to help them prepare, so we lost a hundred years going backwards. We'll never know how high a price we paid for the unkindness and injustice we've inflicted on people—the

Negroes, Mexicans, and Jews—and everyone who really believes he has been discriminated against in any way is part of that great human price. And that cost exists where many people may not even think it does. No matter how well you may think you know a Negro, if you really know one, there'll come the time when you look at him and see how deep his bitterness is.

But there are thousands of people out there who'll never understand this, people who've worked every day to save up for a week's vacation or a new store and they look around and think they see their tax dollars going to finance a bunch of ungrateful rioters. Why, that's bound to make even a nonprejudiced person angry. Prejudice—you know, my feeling all along has been that prejudice about color is not the big factor. Maybe the Poles do hate the Negroes, but I think fear is the cause of their hatred, not prejudice—anyone who's afraid of losing his job to another man will soon turn to hate that other man. Now I thought when we got unemployment down, we'd eliminated that fear. When I got the tax bill passed in '64, it made such a dent in unemployment I figured we were on our way. And when I got the stock market up and everyone was making money, with wages going up even higher than prices, I figured if there was a time when jealousy wouldn't assert itself, it would be this one. Now I knew that as President I couldn't make people want to integrate their schools or open their doors to blacks, but I could make them feel guilty for not doing it and I believed it was my moral responsibility to do precisely that—to use the moral suasions of my office to make people feel that segregation was a curse they'd carry with them to their graves. This guilt was the only chance we had for holding the backlash in check.

Then when we got that voting rights bill passed, I figured the most constructive thing that could have come to the Negroes would have been to register and vote for the people who'd do a good job for them. And when I met all the time with the heads of the black organizations, I knew I was helping those organizations grow in the eyes of their constituents. Why, if Whitney Young or Roy Wilkins could hang a picture of me on their office walls, shaking hands with them, they'd be in good with their people for some time. And when I appointed Thurgood Marshall to the Supreme Court, I figured he'd be a great example to younger kids. There was probably not a Negro in America who didn't know about Thurgood's appointment. All over America that day Negro parents looked at their children a little differently, thousands of mothers looked across the breakfast table and said, "Now maybe this will happen to my child someday." I bet from one coast to the other there was a rash of new mothers naming their newborn sons Thurgood.

Johnson's thoughts and opinions of black Americans' reactions reflect the era of his development and growth in a white society. Even so, his support of civil rights legislation in the 1960s took courage because he knew southern whites would regard him a traitor to the cause of white supremacy. For that reason, he deserves credit for attempting to understand black people's anger and attempting to amend and enforce laws that blacks should have routinely exercised as American citizens. President Johnson is the last of the seven incredible Americans highlighted in this book because of their effort to erase the stain of white supremacy from the Constitution.

The incredible men on the front cover of this book moved the country closer to the founding purpose of the Declaration of

Independence. And the cost in terms of bloodshed, property damage, and relations between the black and white races were high. Each legislative change to the Constitution involved long-standing practices of racial inequality toward blacks that required the white majority to accept. All were met with white resistance requiring the executive, legislative, and judicial branches of government to enforce the Constitutional rights denied to black Americans. There are many lessons here, and one of the most profound is the power of one man who believed that all men are created equal changed America.

Chief Justice Earl Warren's ability to garner a unanimous decision of the associate justices to stop the "separate but equal" public school policy for black students is worth studying and learning the lesson. First, Warren told the justices that *Plessy* (separate but equal) policy was based on racial segregation and the belief that blacks were inferior. He did not believe that, and neither did the Declaration of Independence. Two, in a democracy that values individual freedoms, individuals must be free to choose their beliefs, friends, careers, etc., and public schools in communities where children learn basic education and about each other. Third, to racially integrate public or private institutions requires preparation, education, and time. Four, elected and appointed officials over the three branches of government who don't believe that "all men/people are created equal" enable resisters and prolong institutional racism in America. This is a timeless lesson for maintaining a democracy that works for all of its people. This is a lesson we all must remember when voting for candidates to represent our local, state, and in our three branches of the federal government.

As a personal tribute to the Patriotic Seven, my life's journey and accomplishments summarized in the introduction would not have been possible without the full protection and privileges of the US Constitution. Citizenship, access to public facilities, and voting rights are fundamentally important, but the great equalizer in a democracy is education—education in a multiracial setting is a multiplier for good citizenship. The integration of public schools in 1954 has been the greatest influence in providing young Americans opportunities to develop their interests and abilities in our multicultural society. For over sixty-five years, American youth in public schools have learned basic and technical skills in classrooms that reflect all racial and ethnic residents of the community. They have formed opinions of each other, good and bad, made friends and choices that carried them into adult life. America was changed for the better because of Earl Warren's Supreme Court decision. My experience.

My life was also changed for the better because of my attendance and graduation from Monroe City High School in 1955–1956. At the time, I was not happy to leave all black Douglass High School in Hannibal, Missouri, and experienced some anxiety about being one of a few black students in Monroe City High School. Thanks to basketball coach, Billy Key, and Mrs. Rice Maupin, music teacher, I was pushed to compete in their programs. As a result, I gained self-assurance of my ability to compete in the predominantly white institutions that would become my life's résumé. I also made friends whom I remain in contact with during class reunions and occasional visits in the area. I'm pleased to end this section with the observation that Billy Key and Earl Warren had a lot in common. And in the next and last section, I share my thoughts on what you can do to stop institutional racism and move America closer to her founding purpose.

PART IV

What You Can Do to Stop American Institutional Racism

THIS IS THE LAST AND most telling hard truth that informs and clouds our understanding of American racism. White colonialist severed political ties with white Europeans because of despotism—a list of injustices that ranged from taxation without representation to denial of personal freedoms. Under the tyranny of racism, the American founders withheld the freedoms from enslaved Africans while establishing a philosophical liberal and republican form of government where the leaders governed with consent of the governed. Yet despite announcing to the world that America believed that all men were created equal with certain unalienable rights, the founders continued slavery and treated enslaved Africans and Native Americans worse than the British treated the colonialists.

Racism grew with each passing year, and slavery expanded with new states pledging allegiance to the founding principles. The Civil War came, the confederate states lost the war, and Abraham Lincoln borrowed freely from the Declaration of Independence to refocus the nation on a new beginning. He freed the enslaved Africans in southern states controlled by the union. It was also a gesture that can be interpreted to reconcile the nation's belief that all men were created equal. The tension between the Declaration of Independence and the US Constitution was on full display over the granting of rights of citizenship to the newly freed Africans.

The consent of the governed to accept the Thirteenth, Fourteenth, and Fifteenth Amendments that freed the slaves and protecting their rights as Americans was strongly resisted even among some northern states; the southern states in rebellion had to agree to the amendments as a condition of reentry into the union. The long and tortuous road to bring the consent of the governed (majority white) to accept the inclusion of African Americans, Native Americans, and other minorities as equals under the US Constitution began with President Abraham Lincoln. The most significant gains for blacks and minorities were pushed by Truman, Eisenhower, Kennedy, Johnson, and Justices Warren and Marshall. Institutional racism continues to be the great challenge without a champion.

It only takes one American, strategically positioned, of unquestioned morals and character, and with courage enough to speak her convictions to change the course of history. Lincoln was the first president to recognize that "The whole is greater than the sum of its parts," meaning that he recognized that America would be stronger when the different races are connected together to form one nation. Lincoln and the presidents and supreme court justices on the front cover of this book knew the power of white supremacy because they all were shaped by it. They also knew or learned that the consent of the governed (the white majority) had to be pushed beyond their comfort zone to allow American citizens of other racial or ethnic groups to enjoy the same rights and freedoms accorded them as Americans. The contributions of these seven Americans, whom I call the Patriotic Seven, help us understand the power of America when the connections between its citizens are not separated by boundaries of race, gender, religion, sexual orientation, or age. My optimism of stopping American institutional racism is encouraged by the gains of the beneficiaries (primarily African Americans) of the 1954 Supreme Court integration of public schools, of which I am a member.

This section is where I will deliver on my big bold promise to say about what you can do to stop American institutional racism. I didn't realize how audacious that promise sounded until Carol, a seat companion on a Southwest Airline flight on Veterans Day 2019, from Houston to Las Vegas, appeared stunned at the enormity of my project when I told her the title of the book. While listening to her encouragement, I realized for the first time how incredulous it must sound for one noncelebrity American to believe that his life experience and insight can provide a remedy for 320 million Americans to stop institutional racism. Being of sound mind and an eighty-one-year fairly healthy body, I am compelled to share the source of my audacious belief.

The source of my inspiration is a public service poster promoting free speech and savings bonds in 1942, and the courageous act of my father, Eddie Scott, the only African American attending the white school board meeting in Hunnewell, Missouri, around the same time frame. My dad was asking for a black school to be continued for his children and other black children in the small rural racially segregated town. The black school was continued until 1945.

The poster is a lithograph print of a Norman Rockwell drawing of a man dressed in jacket and working-class clothes, standing to speak among a seated crowd of men dressed in suits with neckties all gazing in approval of his right to speak. All the men in the poster are white males, but as an American of African descent, I identify with the point and have always believed in the right to speak your peace no matter the odds. Equally supportive of my audacious effort is my faith in the Holy Spirit. Most of the opportunities that opened for me during my journey exceeded my expectations and the accomplishments of any American I know from my socioeconomic status, gender, or geographical region; my story is reason to believe that the Holy Spirit works through people to promote God's purpose on earth.

My task is to share my perception of racial attitudes of white Americans who collectively pose the greatest challenge to accept the self-evident truths that unite us as Americans. I approach the task from experience and observation. I recognize that my generalizations of racial group attitudes are more aligned with the racial attitudes of Americans born before 1990. WWII, Civil Rights, and Vietnam events shaped the attitudes of my era and were influx but remained pretty consistent among racial groups during that time period. The attitudes of Americans born after 1990 were shaped by the end of the Cold War, start of the Gulf War, and September 11, 2001, terrorist attacks. These events shifted American racial attitudes from black/white to middle eastern/terrorism. More importantly, significant inclusion of minority participation with whites in education, sports, and the workforce eased racial tensions between all Americans of that era. My perception is that racial diversity and inclusion among this later group of Americans continues without major tensions over race. They are preoccupied with living the American dream and don't appear to think about the self-evident truths or what unites them as Americans.

White and black Americans of my era harbor racial attitudes toward each other that continue to push the white supremacy versus self-evident truths of struggle into the twenty-first century. We older Americans have seen significant changes for the better in America's embrace of the self-evident truths, and my goal is to champion Americans, white, black, and people of color to continue the fight against institutional racism.

White supremacy and the institution of slavery was changed because the words in the Declaration of Independence moved the Patriotic Seven to live up to the meaning of America's founding—the inclusion of all Americans. The antidote to white supremacy can also lead us to end institutional racism.

The next two chapters challenge white Americans to lead the country in the application of the self-evident truths and end institutional racism. The white majority (born before 1990) has its own internal struggles because of the persistent efforts of white nationalists to exclude minorities and promote institutional racism throughout local, state, and federal governments and the judicial system. The consent of the governed has said no to the white supremacist among the white majority since the 1960s and are now challenged to say no to Donald Trump and his Republican Party.

Americans collectively have a vested interest in advancing the self-evident truths while continuing to build strong public and private institutions and organizations that are representative of all Americans. The divisiveness among Americans, and white Americans in particular, make the 2020 presidential election a referendum on choosing a candidate who believes in the self-evident truths or in white supremacy. Trump supporters are not bashful in their support of his policies. Those who believe in the self-evident truths must stand up, speak out, and vote.

We must ensure that the Declaration of Independence shapes the consent of the governed against the ill effects of white supremacy and institutional racism. The simple and most effective way is to vote for candidates who believe in the ideology of individualism and meritocracy across boundaries of race, gender, class, or sexual orientation, and to select the candidate who will govern in the best interest of all Americans at home and abroad.

Throughout this book, I have directed my comments primarily to the white majority. I have learned to be comfortable among a group of white people but recognize there are group dynamics or shared feelings white people may have about race that I may not understand. I know that talking about race, discrimination, prejudice, and white supremacy are difficult. I have seen the pained look on the face of white friends when the subject is introduced. We had no choice in being born into the racial group of our birth, but the choice of our behavior and beliefs are wholly ours. We are not responsible for another person's behavior but are obligated to oppose behavior that threatens the safety, dignity, or self-evident truths of others promised under the Declaration of Independence.

Throughout the next two chapters, I generously borrowed suggestions from Robin DiAngelo, author of *White Fragility*. Robin is a noted sociologist who specializes in race relations. She is up front as to why she wrote her book. "This book is unapologetically rooted in identity politics. I am white and am addressing a common white dynamic. I am mainly writing to a white audience; when I use the terms *us* and *we*. I am referring to the white collective." Robin believes that white people don't see institutional racism because of their belief in the ideology of individualism and meritocracy. I agree with most of her observations and especially her assertion that the white majority only see themselves as the norms for American society and minorities as outside of their norms, and that white people are always the majority in public, private, or corporate setting and never are required to adjust to other cultural or ethnic norms. Robin urges white people to examine their discomfort around minority members so they, too, may learn different perspectives minority members carry to the conversation. I urge you to read Robin's book. Her views, like yours and my own, are important for understanding the corrosive effects of institutional racism in America.

CHAPTER EIGHT

Americans and the Way Forward: Self-Evident Truths…or White Supremacy

THE FOUNDERS OF AMERICA INTRODUCED the self-evident truths as the foundation of their beliefs on founding a new country. They had to know that African slaves were human. In my wildest imagination, I have not been able to understand how a member of the human race could have been excluded from their self-evident truth about the creation of all men. These were intelligent men. Yet the enslaved Africans were excluded from the proclamation. President Abraham Lincoln recognized the humanity of the enslaved Africans when he issued the proclamation of freedom that led to the passage of the Thirteenth, Fourteenth, and Fifteenth Amendments that made the founders' self-evident truths representative of all Americans.

The founders' adoption of *E pluribus unum*, "Out of many, one," as the motto of the Great Seal of the United States in 1782, aptly described the European Americans being easily integrated at that time and the more difficult integration of enslaved Africans, Native Americans, and people of color beginning in the 1860s. Now the motto applies to people from every nation on earth who are citizens of the United States of America. In 2020, Americans are faced with another challenge to remain on the path of self-evident truths or to revert to the pursuit of white supremacy and possibly autocracy. This is a new and frightening development!

The American voters and especially white voters will have to decide in favor of the self-evident truths or Donald Trump's brand of white nationalism and autocratic leadership. The decision requires an understanding of white supremacy, prejudice, institutional racism, and whiteness. Some or all of these racial attitudes influence the collective white majority. So much so, that white Americans are now confronted with a white racial ideology based on loyalty to Donald Trump's Republican Party as the dividing line between white Americans. The information that follows is intended to help white Americans identify the racial attitudes toward black and minority Americans that contributed to our past and current crisis. Institutional racism can't be stopped without knowing and understanding how and why it is embedded in the white socialization process.

As I write this book in 2020, the country is divided over the impeachment of President Trump for high crimes and misdemeanors. The divisiveness between Republicans and Democrats in the house and senate is not likely to result in impeachment, leaving the American people to resolve the issue of Trump's fitness to continue as president in the 2020 presidential election. Many of the racial attitudes addressed below will be on display in support of Trump and lead his followers to ignore or discredit the importance of the self-evident truths in the Declaration of Independence and Constitution of the United States.

I respect the sovereignty of your vote and hope that your decision will be informed by the founding principles in the Declaration of Independence and the amendments of the Constitution that govern our rights and privileges. As an American of African descent, I have voluntarily risked my life to support and defend the amended Constitution of the United States against all enemies, foreign and domestic, and am still prepared to defend our hard-won freedoms. I hope you, too, are prepared to do the same.

The self-evident truths in the Declaration is the lifeline that binds us together and makes America unique on planet earth. You have not had to cope with being black in America, and I have not had the experience of being white in America. However, the information shared about white racial attitudes is intended to be helpful and is extracted from my experience and the professional studies and observations of Robin DiAngelo, a white sociologist and author of *White Fragility*. Robin provides a fair definition of racism and prejudice for all races. Excerpts below from her specific explanations of white people, white supremacy, and whiteness are based on her sociological studies. Her research of white racial attitudes toward black and people of color are useful for those who want to stop institutional racism. More importantly, these excerpts may be useful in your thoughts and decisions in the exercise of your vote for the 2020 presidential election. The stakes are high, and Americans will decide either in favor of the self-evident truths or some form of white nationalism or autocracy.

Excerpts: "Racism, White Supremacy, Whiteness" from Robin DiAngelo's White Fragility

Racism is a social construct created to justify unequal treatment.

> The beneficiaries of slavery, segregation, and mass incarceration have reproduced racist ideas of Black people being best suited for or deserving of the confines of slavery, segregation, or the jail cell. Consumers of these racist ideas have been led to believe there is something wrong with Black people, and not the policies that have enslaved, oppressed, and confined so many Black people.
>
> —Ibram Kendi, historian,
> *Stamped from the Beginning*

Racism differs from prejudice and discrimination. All humans have prejudices and discriminate against people, places or things.

> Prejudice is pre-judgement about another person based on the social groups to which that person belongs. Prejudice consists of thoughts and

110

feelings, including stereotypes, attitudes and generalizations that are based on little or no experience and then are projected onto everyone from that group. Our prejudices tend to be shared because we swim in the same cultural water and absorb the same messages.

—DiAngelo

When a racial group's collective prejudice is backed by the power of legal authority and institutional control, it is transformed into racism, a far-reaching system that functions independently from the intentions or self-images of individual actors.

—J. Kehaulani Kauanui, professor of American studies and anthropology at Wesleyan University, explains, "Racism is a structure, not an event."

Whiteness:

Being perceived as white carries more than a mere racial classification; it is a social and institutional status and identity imbued with legal, political, economic, and social rights and privileges that are denied to others.

—DiAngelo

Tracing the evolving concept of whiteness as property, race scholar Cheryl Harris explains,

By according whiteness and actual legal status, an aspect of identity was converted into an external object of property, moving whiteness from privileged identity to a vested interest. The law's construction of whiteness defined and affirmed critical aspects of identity (who is white); of privilege (what benefits accrue to that status); and, of property (what legal entitlements arise from that status). Whiteness at various times signifies and is deployed as identity, status, and property, sometimes singularly, sometimes in tandem.

White supremacy: Most white people do not identify with images of white supremacists and take great umbrage to the term being used more broadly.

> Race scholars use the term white supremacy to describe a sociopolitical economic system of domination based on racial categories that benefit those defined and perceived as white. This system of structural power privileges, centralizes, and elevates white people as a group.
>
> —DiAngelo

White resistance to the term *white supremacy* prevents the term from being studied and allows radical groups to align with main stream groups without public alarm. Explicit white supremacist understands the advantage of mainstream alignment.

> Christian Picciolini, a former white nationalist, explains that white nationalists recognized that they had to distance themselves from the terms racist and white supremacy to gain broader appeal. He describes the "alt-right" and white nationalist movements as the culmination of a thirty-year effort to massage the white supremacist message: We recognized back then that we were turning away the average American white racists and that we needed to look and speak more like our neighbors. The idea was to blend in, normalize, make the message more palatable.
>
> —DiAngelo

Birth of the Southern Strategy: In a 1981 interview, Lee Atwater, Republican political strategist and adviser to presidents Ronald Regan and George H.W. Bush, explained how to appeal to the racism of white Southern voters without pronouncing it openly. "You start out in 1954 by saying, 'Nigger, nigger, nigger.' By 1968 you can't say 'nigger'—that hurts you. Backfires. So, you say stuff like forced busing, states' rights and all that stuff. You're getting so abstract now [that] you're talking about cutting taxes, and all these things are totally economic things and a byproduct of them is [that] blacks get hurt worse than whites. And subconsciously maybe that is part of it... But I'm saying that it is getting that abstract, and that coded, that we are doing away with the racial problem one way or the other. You follow me because obviously sitting around saying, "We want to cut this," is much more abstract than even the busing thing, and a hell of a lot more abstract than "Nigger, nigger."

—DiAngelo

Why name white supremacy?

Naming white supremacy changes the conversation in two key ways. It makes the system visible and shifts the locus of change onto white people, where it belongs. It also points us in the direction of the lifelong work that is uniquely ours, challenging our complicity with and investment in racism. This does not mean that people of color do not play a part but that the full weight of responsibility rests with those who control the institutions.

—DiAngelo

Do you see a mirror or a window while reading the above?

The excerpts are unique to white Americans and explain the ratio-nale behind the why and how institutional racism still exists. White racial attitudes dominate the American political agenda and hold the key to the future. Black and minority attitudes are important and are consistently in favor of the self-evident principles of inclusion in the nation's progress, but people of color don't have the power to stop insti-tutional racism. Like-minded Americans have the power to stop it.

According to DiAngelo in "why name white supremacy" above, white people created institutional racism and are complicit in passing it from one generation to the next and therefore have the responsibility to stop it. The question may be, why should white Americans stop institutional racism? The obvious answer is that rac-ism promotes domestic turmoil. The lynching and brutality against black Americans in the 1800s and early 1900s, and the burning and destruction of property during the riots of the mid 1960s, are the bitter fruits of white supremacy. Domestic tranquility has been a hallmark of racial integration since the 1980s, and most Americans want to keep it that way.

The better answer for stopping institutional racism is that the surest way to maintain domestic tranquility and promote prosperity is to replace institutional racism with institutional meritocracy through diversity. However, the presidency of Donald Trump is a threat to domestic tranquility and a nod toward white nationalism. Trump must be removed from office so that America can continue with institutional meritocracy that was started over the past forty years under Republican and Democrat administrations. Unfortunately, Trump is a diversion from moving forward, and I must enlist your support now before continuing with the benefits of the self-evident truths and institutional meritocracy. Will you help?

Why You Should Leave the Comfort of Whiteness to Promote the Self-Evident Truths of the Declaration of Independence

White American voters with the courage to tackle racism can resolve the Trump crisis and move the country forward with institutional meritocracy. My guess is that if you are white and reading this book, you are more likely to identify with the Democratic Party. If you are a Republican or an independent and reading this book, you are probably not a die-hard Trump fan and therefore may be a candidate to become a proponent of self-evident truths of America. In either case, as a white Democrat, Republican, or independent, you are probably not eager to confront racism, but I hope you will have the courage to try. Democracy as we have known it is at risk, and we all must do what we can to elect a president who believes and promotes the self-evident truths in the Declaration of Independence. Here's how you can help.

You probably know white Americans who identify themselves as Republicans, Democrats, or independents who support Trump. This is where your courage is needed to bear witness about the importance of supporting the self-evident truths.

The most important test of being an American is subordinating ethnicity to nationality. We are born in a country that asks us to look beyond our skin color, hair texture, and eye shape, to discover our common nationality where we can live, work, and use our talents for ourselves, our family, friends, and our community.

Americans have created a universal culture where we have the freedom to choose our mate, profession or work, religion or be an atheist, and use public facilities without worry for our personal safety because of our ethnicity, race, or economic status. Sporting and entertainment events commonly host large crowds of racially diverse fans without incidents, and racially integrated teams select players based on talent and performance. This multiracial culture was made possible because the men featured on the front cover of this book and the hundreds of thousands who died made the self-evident truths a reality of the American experience. We must take pride in the humanity of Americans of all races and especially Abraham Lincoln, Harry Truman, Earl Warren, and the rest who had the courage to create the culture just described. These white Americans, elected and appointed to the highest offices in the country, validated that the self-evident truths apply to all persons fortunate enough to be an American citizen. These men subordinated their whiteness, racial prejudice, and privileged status to demonstrate that America is one nation, under God, with liberty and justice for all. This is why we all must follow their lead in 2020 and vote for the candidate who will secure the self-evident truths.

Thanks in advance for doing your part to keep America true to her DNA: the self-evident truths in the Declaration of Independence. You will have many opportunities to hear Trump supporters, associates, or friends who claim to be independents and those who don't think their vote matters. No one is likely to bring up racism because those who favor white nationalism have developed code issues that target blacks and people of color without having to sound racist. Welfare and entitlement programs are favorite topics and have become code words for people of color. Other popular distractions will center around liberalism, socialism, and invading criminals and drug dealers crossing our southern border. You probably have answers or opinions on those common divisive issues. However, regardless of your or their persuasive arguments on hot-button issues, our goal must be to elect a president who will abide by the Constitution and pursue the important issues confronting the American people. The hot-button issues cannot be allowed to dismiss the autocratic use of power for the president's political or personal gain, or his override of defense department leaders who don't agree with his personal goals or interference in matters of military justice. Trump's autocratic leadership has also paralyzed executive branch departments and turned the Republican Party into a cult. In my opinion, these developments undermine American democratic principles and are far more important than hot-button issues. Having a democracy to decide hot-button issues is far more important than having an autocracy announcing the outcome of hot-button issues. And to get back to a democracy and continue on the path toward inclusive governance, we must examine the record of past administrations and choose wisely.

The forty years prior to Trump's presidency, Democrat and Republican administrations established a clear record of their emphasis on governance. You may find the results useful in your chats with Trump Republicans or others who don't see or embrace the self-evident truths in the governance of America.

The Politics of Democrats and Republicans, 1980–Present: Self-Evident Truths (Inclusion) versus Divisiveness and Identity Politics

The Bush and Clinton administrations (1980–2001) supported and encouraged the complete restructuring of military recruitment, retention, development, and promotion policies that made the military services the most respected and racially diverse institution in America. The Defense Equal Opportunity Management Institute established in 1971 continues to help the military services maintain meritocracy through racial diversity. Racial diversity is the norm throughout the services living, training, deployment, and command structure. Meritocracy is the basis of selection for schooling and promotions throughout the Department of Defense. The military is a great example of a system formerly maintained by institutional racism that seriously tested military discipline and order during the late stages of the Vietnam War. The US Army led the services in establishing institutional diversity through meritocracy.

In less than three years, Trump has disrupted the continuity of leadership at the Defense Department with so many top leaders resigning, including General Mattis, the former Secretary of Defense, that we Americans don't know the number of vacancies in each of the services. We do know that the secretary of the navy resigned because the president pardoned a Navy SEAL over the objection of the admirals in the chain of command. We also know that a recent poll of military service members showed that nearly 50 percent of military service members have an unfavorable view of the commander-in-chief, President Trump. This should be an alarming development for Americans because our service members are all volunteers and make up less than one-tenth of 1 percent of Americans who serve in our military services. Thankfully American generals, admirals, and officers swear an oath to support and defend the constitution of the United States. While they serve at the pleasure of the president, I am confident that they will honor the oath until fired by the president.

* * *

William Jefferson Clinton, Democrat (1993–2001)

Clinton appointed more minority cabinet members (five African American and three Hispanic) than any president in history. The National and Community Service Trust Act, created by President Clinton in 1993, incorporated VISTA (Volunteers in Service to America) and the National Civilian Community Corps (NCCC) and a third division, AmeriCorps State and National, and provide grants to hundreds of local community organizations throughout the United States. More than eighty thousand Americans participate in community service activities annually. I was appointed by President Clinton as the founding director of the NCCC, AmeriCorps flagship residential program that recruits eighteen to twenty-four-year-olds to volunteer for a ten-month service tour. The racially diverse teams perform disaster relief operations and community-sponsored projects from educational assistance to environmental restoration. The successful model is used by the Federal Emergency Management Agency to create their own disaster relief teams. The oath AmeriCorps members take and live by is a model of civic responsibility:

> I will get things done for America-to make our
> People safer, smarter, and healthier
> I will bring Americans together to strengthen our
> Communities.
> Faced with apathy, I will take action.
> Faced with conflict, I will seek common ground.
> Faced with adversity, I will persevere.
> I will carry this commitment with me this year
> and beyond.
> I am an AmeriCorps member, and I will get
> things done.

This Democrat initiative promotes the self-evident truths and uses selection criteria that promotes team work and civic responsibility through meritocracy and diversity.

Barack Hussein Obama II, Democrat (2009–2017)

He's the first multiracial president of the United States. According to Gallup poll, December 2018, "Obama was just one first-place finish short of tying Dwight Eisenhower for the most times being Most Admired Man. Eisenhower won the distinction 12 times—the eight years he was president from 1953 through 1960, as well as in 1950, 1952, 1967 and 1968." Obama won the distinction the eight years of his presidency, 2017, and tied with Donald Trump for the distinction in 2018 and 2019. President Obama, despite his popularity and outstanding achievements to restore Wall Street's credibility and the American automobile industry during a downturn in the American economy, was under constant racial attack from conservative Republicans. Senator Mitch McConnel, Republican, Kentucky, vowed not to cooperate with any legislation initiated by Obama that would help the American people. Donald Trump, aspiring and later candidate elected to the presidency of the US, pushed the lie that Obama was not born in the United States. Radio talk show host Rush Limbaugh also used his popular platform to attack President Obama's credibility. Notwithstanding the attacks, the Democratic Party's election of President Obama was in the greatest tradition of American realization of self-evident truths.

Donald John Trump (2017–present)

Republican lost the popular vote but won the most electoral votes to win the presidency. He promised to make America great again and build a wall on the southern border that Mexico would pay for. He has been described as a populist, protectionist, and nationalist. Many of his comments and actions have been characterized as racially charged or racist. Donald Trump defeated sixteen candidates in the primaries and capitalized on Regan's Southern Strategy. Ronald Regan developed the Southern Strategy to lure Democrats to vote Republican in 1980. The strategy worked eight years for Regan, four years for H. W. and eight years for G. W. Bush, and eight years for Senator Mitch McConnel, who successfully resisted senate action to support the country during the Obama administration. Lee Atwater's subtle attacks against African Americans in the 1980s have now become open chants against Hispanic Americans led by Donald Trump to predominantly white audiences in the south, border states, and white Rust Belt workers in northern states. White receptivity to Trump's message suggests that they are attracted to the racist message despite his unpresidential behavior, lying, and defiance of the constitution. Trump's policies support institutional racism in cabinet appointments, support of republican candidates for political offices at all governmental levels, and in his influence over the nearly all white Republican Party. The current Republican Party acts, speaks, and looks like a party that does not embrace the self-evident truths of the Declaration of Independence.

* * *

White Americans who self-identify as political independents once again find themselves in the middle and are usually blamed as spoilers against the Republican or Democrat candidate. Now is the time to choose to support the Democratic Party. In the past, both Democratic and Republican Parties promoted policies favorable to white Americans. No loss of freedoms was at stake. Trump and his Republican Party appear to play by a white nationalist set of rules that could border on autocracy with support of Trump's ideology (whatever it is) being the price of freedom. White voters under Trump are either with him or against him. Democracy as experienced before Trump is at risk. Remaining a political independent in 2020 presidential election advantages white supremacy, nationalism, or whatever Trump decides to name it.

The Self-Evident Truths Are the Most Powerful Argument for America and Americans

The importance of DiAngelo's book and my message is not race but the inclusion of all races that make up America. The self-evident truths included all humanity created by God (the practice of slavery did not alter the fact). Racism is a barrier that prevents Americans from cultivating the best and brightest from all ethnic, racial, social, gender, and cultural backgrounds to solve American problems. The most important result of the civil rights struggles is learning that the self-evident truths work best for America when meritocracy through diversity is the basis for leading and staffing institutions. A racially diverse government, corporation, financial institution, educational institution can best serve the needs and problems of a racially diverse country. Beneath the acquired education and training received at schools and universities is a foundation of perceptions gained from our ethnic or cultural birth group. When diverse teams of well qualified Americans tackle a problem, they bring solutions appropriate to the people and their needs. White Americans who want to remove the barriers of race from leading and staffing institutions (destroying institutional racism) must be willing to get out of their racial comfort zone.

Getting Out of Your Racial Comfort Zone Broadens Perspective and Serves the Self-Evident Truths of America

Minority Americans are required to abandon their comfort zone to learn the culture of the institution, corporation, organization, or business that is usually led and staffed by white Americans. Dress, manners, customs, and expressions can be mastered, but interpersonal relationships take much longer to establish. Most white people have not worked with black or minority people but have heard opinions that characterize the racial group. Barriers are usually breached by sharing family problems, concerns, and celebrations and discovering mutual likes and dislikes over a meal. As the minority member advances in competence and promotions, her reputation as a team player and problem solver precedes her leadership of the enterprise. At this point, race is no longer an issue. The minority leader is comfortable in his own skin, whether among his, a mixed, or as a minority in another racial group.

White Americans should take advantage of opportunities to be a minority among people of color. The experience broadens awareness of how minorities view common problems with a different perspective. It may also produce a change in the perspective of the white person about people of color. For Christians, a good experience is to visit a predominately black church within the same denomination. Being the only white person among a sea of black or brown persons produces its own internal emotions while trying to absorb the spiritual message. The experience will be useful in efforts to stop institutional racism and promote diversity through meritocracy. Other safe venues can be selected with the help of a member of a black organization like the NAACP, Urban League, museum, or minority on the city council or county representative.

White Americans bear the major responsibility for both the good and the ills of America. The American presidents on the cover of this book have enforced the changes in the constitution that produced the inclusiveness that we now experience. All the presidents up to Donald Trump have continued efforts to make the self-evident truths apply to all Americans. Your help will assure that Americans elect a person of character, integrity, and loyalty to the constitution and self-evident truths of the Declaration of Independence.

CHAPTER NINE

What You Can Do to Stop Institutional Racism

1. Accept the fact that white Americans created America by taking the land from Native Americans and placed them on reservations, enslaved Africans, freed the Africans, and created racial barriers that endured and continue as institutional racism. The vestiges of slavery and racism created the intercity slums. The intercity schools and marginal living conditions are the result of slavery and years of institutional racism. See 6 below.

2. Internalize and govern your behavior on the self-evident truths in the Declaration of Independence:

    Declaration of Independence: A Transcription
    In Congress, July 4, 1776.

    The unanimous Declaration of the thirteen United States of America, When in the Course of human events, it becomes necessary for one people to dissolve the political bands which have connected them with another, and to assume among the powers of the earth, the separate and equal station to which the Laws of Nature and of Nature's God entitle them a decent respect to the opinions of mankind requires that they should declare the causes which impel them to the separation.

We hold these truths to be self-evident, that all men are created equal, that they are endowed by their Creator with certain unalienable Rights, that among these are Life, Liberty and the pursuit of Happiness... (The text is a transcription of the stone engraving of the parchment of Declaration of Independence, the document on display in the Rotunda at the National Archives Museum.)

3. Christians preach, teach, and practice the teachings of Jesus Christ. Drop the adjective *white*, *black*, *Korean*, or *evangelical* before Christian, and do what Christ commanded us to do.

4. Elected and appointed city, county, state, and federal officials, be faithful to 2 above and the oath of office you swear to obey. Model civility, promote principles of honesty, integrity, and equal justice to your constituents. Place American nationality over your ethnicity. Replace institutional racism with meritocracy in the hiring and staffing of employees. This is best accomplished by hiring reputable firms that provide a racially diverse pool of highly qualified candidates to meet your needs. In areas with a large and racially diverse population, pick candidates to ensure the government is representative of the population it serves.

5. Chambers of Commerce, city, regional, state, and federal, internalize 2 above and encourage members in large racially diverse areas to hire diverse staff and to include people of color in their marketing ads. People of color, like the majority population, have people with disposable income to invest and spend. The more inclusive a target population, the greater the potential revenue. People of color prefer to spend with companies that have a racially diverse business.

6. School boards, parents, teachers, and community leaders. Public schools remain the best source of preparation,
mobility, socialization, and hope for America's future.
Great teachers, equal resourcing, and multiracial students
are a likely formula for success. Intercity schools are the
exception and are a crisis getting worse. Most intercity
schools have reverted to the previous all-black, separate,
and unequal status, of the pre-1954 Supreme Court
decision outlawing separate but equal schools. The solution lies outside of the resources and abilities of the city
and state to fix. The federal government in partnership
with the city and state can and must find a way to hire
well-qualified teachers, resource the schools, and provide a
nonburdensome cross-racial learning environment for the
students. This is a 243-year ongoing problem exacerbated
by slavery and institutional racism. Forced bussing is not
viable; relocation of residents isn't either. Redevelopment
of the intercity is the surest and best way to resolve this
problem. The late mayor Maynard Jackson of Atlanta,
Georgia, used to talk about redeveloping neighborhoods
with mixed (socioeconomic) housing as the most viable
way to get rid of blighted neighborhoods. The planned
neighborhoods consisted of middle-income single family
homes and low-income single family homes interspersed
throughout the development. The idea is worth pursu-
ing as an element of a larger redevelopment scheme to
add job-producing businesses, transportation, and other
incentives to make city living attractive to a racially diverse
population. The objective is to provide communities with
a tax base with living and work opportunities to sustain
good schools for children—the future of America.

7. Community leaders and volunteers who preserve local and
regional historical events of national significance, institutional racism shaped the attitudes, housing developments,
work, schooling, worship, and social opportunities of the
towns, cities, and regions of America. Institutional rac-

ism divided communities on the basis of race, and even after passage of civil and equal rights laws ending racial segregation, racist attitudes continued to influence the separation of residents on the basis of race. Leaders and volunteers who preserve these sites provide perspectives that can help communities bridge racial attitudes and promote understanding between residents of different ethnic backgrounds. Freedoms Frontier National Heritage Area (FFNHA) in Missouri and Kansas and Jim's Journey in Hannibal, Missouri, are good examples of making past institutional racist practices/events relevant to present residents and visitors.

FFNHA, headquartered in Lawrence, Kansas, covers the historical events that occurred in the twenty-nine counties of Kansas's eastern border and the nineteen counties on Missouri's western border during the border war and Civil War years; it also includes the Monroe School building, Topeka, Kansas, that was the school used to overturn segregation in public schools in the 1954 Supreme Court decision.

Hannibal, Missouri, the home of Mark Twain, features the Huck Finn Freedom Center and Jim's Journey, the African American museum that hosts school children and visitors to explain the life and times of the city's black community during racial segregation. The site has become a collaborative place for interracial gatherings and is an added attraction for the city's tourist trade.

There are fifty-five National Heritage Areas, and every state and most counties have historical societies. Leaders and volunteers of these cultural sites need help from minority members of their communities to make the past relevant to the future.

The Rationale for the Seven Actions and Concluding Comments

The first action required to stop institutional racism is to accept the fact that slavery and institutional racism is the cause of black concentration and poverty in urban intercities. The consent of the governed was complicit in the approval of slavery for nearly ninety years, and following emancipation, the voters sanctioned Jim Crow and separate but equal laws for another one hundred years. Armed with that fact, the six categories of American citizens above, who strongly believe in the proposition that Americans are created equal and endowed by their creator with the unalienable rights to life, liberty, and the pursuit of happiness, can stop institutional racism in America.

The most important person in America is the individual citizen voter. Under the American system of governance, she or he is created equal in the sight of God, and their vote is equal to all others under the laws of the constitution. When like-minded citizens band together representing the interests of their fellow citizens, the will of the people prevail. I have no doubts of the power like-minded Americans can exercise when they use their God-given rights to vote for a just and prosperous America.

The survey of American racism and the changes for racial inclusion of all Americans reported in this book are also a testament to the will of like-minded Americans. And more important than the will of like-minded Americans are the "Laws of Nature and of Nature's God" that the founders invoked in the Declaration of Independence. These laws more easily explain the actions of Abraham Lincoln and Harry Truman, the two presidents who encountered the greatest resistance from the white majority, to change the constitution for inclusion of racial minorities. These laws, more commonly called the will of God, are the mandate for change in America.

My faith in God and his sovereign power to influence behavior leads me to believe that liked-minded individuals working together in the seven areas above can stop institutional racism.

Thanks for reading my book and for having the courage to stop American racism. To paraphrase President Harry Truman, the buck stops with each one of us.